FRED STERN

WORD PROCESSING AND BEYOND

THE INTRODUCTORY COMPUTER BOOK

ILLUSTRATED BY
BETSY JAMES &
PETER ASCHWANDEN

JOHN MUIR PUBLICATIONS

*To Mildred Stern and Heather Stern, my bridges
to the past and future.*

Acknowledgements

This book belongs to Elizabeth Johnson, who in addition to being editor-typist and therapist, provided the moral and economic support to make it a reality. I love you, Betsy.

Appreciation also to Ken Luboff and John Muir Publications, who believe that people can become authors with their first book. And to illustrators Peter Aschwanden and Betsy James.

My thanks to Carol Rowie, the book's first editor, and to the support provided by Deborah Reade, Richard Polese, Paul Abrams and Mr. John Stick of the JMP staff—and, of course, to my dear friend, Eve Muir, the spirit behind John Muir Publications. To Charles M. Thatcher, who tried to teach me about computers in the 1960s. And most importantly to my spiritual teachers, the late Leo Stern and John Muir.

Word
Processing
and
Beyond

INTRODUCTION

The best technical book I ever read, and one that changed my life, was a book written by John Muir and illustrated by Peter Aschwanden: *How to Keep Your Volkswagen Alive: A Manual of Step-by-Step Procedures for the Compleat Idiot.* Like so many of us in the late 60s, I drove nothing but Volkswagens and felt totally incompetent when it came to working on mine. I was an engineering professor who could have easily computed the CO_2 emission on any VW bug, an armchair expert on technology who couldn't repair my own car on a bet. Then along came John's book. The first things that struck me were how enjoyable it was to read and how easy it was to understand, something I had never before experienced in a repair manual.

The "idiot" John wrote the book for was a person like you or me who was finding it virtually impossible to keep up with the rate at which technological changes were being made, a person bogged down by the new language constantly being invented as technology progressed. John could really translate technical jargon into everyday English. He had a rare gift for teaching that made it possible for everyone to be his or her own auto mechanic. Even I, of all people, rebuilt a VW engine with the aid of his book.

John died about a year before John Muir Publications purchased its first computer. The computer sat idle for three years. How in the heck could a company founded on the understanding and teaching of technology purchase a computer and not be able to use it? JMP experienced the same thing that thousands of computer purchasers experience—hour after hour of frustration. The world of the computer is very different from the world of pistons, gears and cylinders. It is a world of strange small plastic rectangles with protruding metal tabs. It is a world that cannot be viewed in the same way as an automobile engine. The digital universe makes the concept of clockwise and counterclockwise obsolete. A digital clock has no hands.

Then one day Ken Luboff called me about doing a JMP book on word processing. I took a trip out to Santa Fe to visit Eve Muir and the JMP family, and deliver an outline for this book. After talking with Ken, Karen, Ada, Joan and the rest of the staff, they offered to give me their machine to write this book. As a matter of fact, they begged me to take it. I accepted, started writing, and even managed to finish a first draft of it, but did the second draft on a fancier machine.

Not only is this book about word processing, it is an introduction to the world of personal computers, a new generation of computing machines designed to be used by John's "idiots" or people with no advanced mathematics or technical training. It is a treat for me to have had the opportunity to write a book that demystifies the world of computers, making them accessible to everyone. Computers have played an important role in my life for more than twenty years. I have seen them evolve from a university research tool to a household appliance. I have used them for scientific research, to create art, to write poetry and now to write this book.

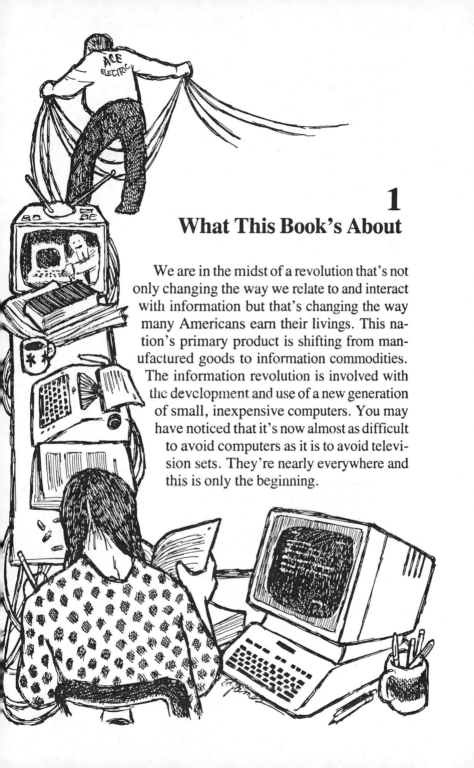

1
What This Book's About

We are in the midst of a revolution that's not only changing the way we relate to and interact with information but that's changing the way many Americans earn their livings. This nation's primary product is shifting from manufactured goods to information commodities. The information revolution is involved with the development and use of a new generation of small, inexpensive computers. You may have noticed that it's now almost as difficult to avoid computers as it is to avoid television sets. They're nearly everywhere and this is only the beginning.

"Wait a minute, why all this talk about computers," you say, "isn't this a book on word processing?" It sure is, and more people use computers to do word processing than to do all other computer-related tasks combined. So, if word processing is the reason most people are using computers, why not start out by learning word processing and then use that skill as an entry into the world of computers beyond word processing? It's like killing two stones with one book.

Some Background

Computers are high-speed machines that assist us in working with two forms of information: numbers and words. A more appropriate name for a computer would be an "information processor," since all computers can work with or process information as words or numbers.

The first computers were used for data processing and worked only with numbers. Data processing includes anything from solving mathematical problems to keeping business accounts. It was in the early data processing days that the image of the computer person as a mathematical genius in a white coat was formed. Or was it in those old science fiction movies?

Using a computer to work with written material is called *text-processing*. The first text processors were called text editors since they were used to write and correct the text of data processing programs.

Word Processing

Now, the use of a computer to help you write and edit anything you might care to write is called word processing. "Ah," you exclaim, "so a word processor is really a computer that works like a super typewriter?" Yes, and it's more than a super typewriter; it's a writing machine that not only lets you type but also edit and store your writing.

"So how does it work?" you ask. The starting point is, of course, the typewriter since the word processor uses a standard typewriter keyboard. Yep, unfortunately in order to use a word processor you have to be able to type. Maybe one finger at a time to start with, but there's no way out of typing, There's good news for those of you who have been doing battle with the typewriter since grade school. Things are about to pick up because many of the writing machines can also help you improve your typing ability in addition to processing your words. These systems can actually instruct you while keeping an eye on your typing skills. I played with one of these and my typing speed doubled after only two lessons. I can now type with two fingers instead of one.

"These machines are great, but what do they cost?" Good question. Like motor vehicles, they cost from $1000 to $100,000 depending on whether you're purchasing the equivalent of a motor-cycle, a Volkswagen, a Mercedes, or an eighteen-wheeler. There's a wide variety of world processing systems available to solve a whole spectrum of writing needs. Just as motor vehicles are similar in their operations, so are most word processors. If you can operate one, it's easy to learn another.

The Great Computer Myth

Have you heard the term *computer literacy?* It is used to imply a level of knowledge or understanding of computer technology. I believe the term was invented and is being promoted by computer manufacturers who are not designing easily usable systems. If computers were designed to be people-literate, there'd be no need for computer literacy.

A people-literate system or machine is one that's designed to be easily used by most people. As an example, let's look at a popular small-scale computer that has had an impact on everyone's life: the calculator. The calculator has changed the way we do arithmetic. It has removed all the insecurities I ever had about adding a column of numbers or carrying out long division. In fact I would not consider doing long division without one. Let's look at some of the attributes of the calculator which enabled it to replace calculation methods used for centuries.

The calculator lets us do arithmetic in the same old way. The only difference: pushing buttons instead of writing numbers. You say 23 times 23 is what? At that point the machine displays the correct answer—529—saving you the time and brainwork of carrying out the operation. The popular acceptance of the calculator is attributable to the following factors:

1. It is simple to use, faster and easier than the old way.
2. It lets you work the same way you normally would.
3. It is accurate and reliable.
4. It is affordable.

Any tool or system we consider using must have these features if we are to use it effectively. This is especially true of people-literate computers.

Using People-Literate Machines

A *fourth-generation* computer system is another name for a people-literate computer system. There have been four stages of evolution from the computer used by the white-coated scientist to the small writing machine that fits on your desk. The first three generations of computers actually required a person to write computer instructions to make the machine do anything. Can you imagine what a calculator would be like if you had to teach it how to do arithmetic before you could use it? Not too pleasant a thought. Fortunately, the calculator was designed to work as a low-level fourth-generation system. Like the calculator, all fourth-generation systems are easy to use and some are even capable of helping you to learn how they operate.

Today's word processing systems are setting new standards for how well computers can be made to interact with people. They have led to the development of other easily usable systems for accounting and business functions, scheduling activities, organizing information and enabling machines to send information to each other.

One thing I have difficulty understanding is why so many of the introductory computer books still talk about the need to *program* in order to use a computer. The whole concept is simply untrue. It is as absurd as saying you need to know how to repair a car in order to drive one.

The Organization of this Book

This book is about choosing and using word processors and computing machines as you would any other appliance. You'll learn about word processing in the same way you learned to drive a car: turn on the key, step on the gas and drive away. Most of us are not interested in knowing how to repair our cars or even the details of how they function. We just want to know how to choose one that runs well. The same is true with a word processor; you want to turn it on and start writing.

Chapters 2 through 6 take you on a guided tour of how to operate a typical word processing system. They present all the information you'll need to know to drive one—excuse me, use one. These chapters let you see what a word processor can do and, even more important, what they can't do. By the end of the section you'll understand some of the language of word processors and computers and how they work.

Chapter 7 describes the *software* (programmed instructions) that actually make word processors process words. You will find cost information as well as a description of the available features.

Chapter 8 is about the other computer-type things you can make your word processor do. I'll discuss the new fourth-generation programs that everyone is talking about. I also share some insight into programming languages, for those of you who want to get into the nitty gritty.

Chapters 9 and 10 describe the different kinds of word processing systems. Here you'll find the detailed descriptions and explanations of word processor and computer component parts and how they function. This is the section where I demystify those computer terms that everyone talks about but few people understand.

Chapters 11 and 12 are a guide for selecting and purchasing your word processor. There's a comprehensive checklist to simplify the selection process as well as lots of advice on financing and purchasing.

Chapter 13, probably the most important chapter in the book, addresses the potential health problems that can result if you work with a word processor under improper conditions. Don't work on a word processor before you've read this chapter!

Chapter 14 contains practical suggestions for installing your system, and presents ways to avoid the things that can cause incredible problems for both you and your machine. It also has a what-to-do-when-problems-happen section.

Chapter 15 explains how information can be sent from one computer to another. You'll learn about electronic mail and publishing, what's available through the information utilities and what's needed to start your own electronic cottage industry.

Chapter 16 tells how to set up word processors and computers for use by more than one person or how to "network" machines. It's also where I pull out my crystal ball and talk about what new developments I see coming down the pike.

There's a glossary of terms, and last but not least are appendices which contain detailed resource lists on just about everything you'll need to select, purchase, and use a fourth-generation writing machine.

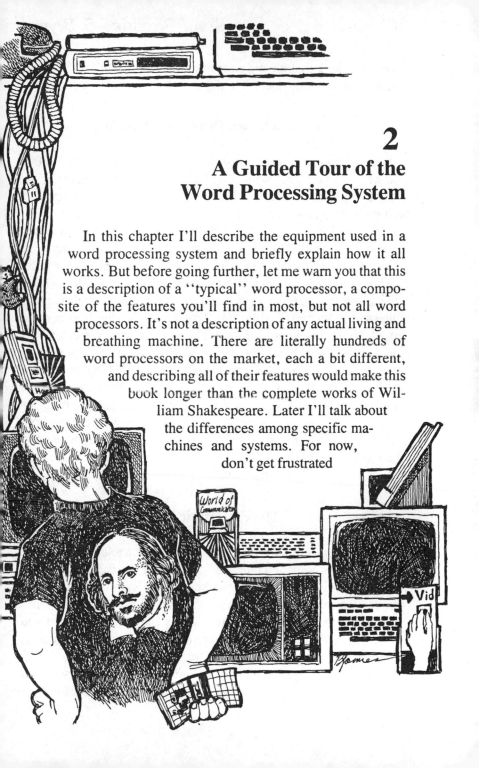

2
A Guided Tour of the Word Processing System

In this chapter I'll describe the equipment used in a word processing system and briefly explain how it all works. But before going further, let me warn you that this is a description of a "typical" word processor, a composite of the features you'll find in most, but not all word processors. It's not a description of any actual living and breathing machine. There are literally hundreds of word processors on the market, each a bit different, and describing all of their features would make this book longer than the complete works of William Shakespeare. Later I'll talk about the differences among specific machines and systems. For now, don't get frustrated if you read here that a word processor has feature "x" and you go out and find one that doesn't.

What is a Word Processing System?

It is a small, relatively low-cost computer ($1,000 to $10,000) that will help you type, write, and edit any kind of written material. Like a typewriter, the machine doesn't care whether you are writing memos, reports, books, or love letters. It just wants to help. At the very least it could be said that word processing is a better way to type. But unlike a typewriter it writes onto an electronic page rather than a piece of paper. Pressing a typewriter key results in a physical mark on a piece of paper. So, a typo or simple revision such as inserting a few words could mean retyping a whole page or unleashing a stream of white-out. To say the least, this is extremely frustrating and time consuming. The word processor's electronic page, on the other hand, lets you move words around, delete parts of what you've written, correct typos and insert things that were left out all before it prints the page on paper. This feature, combined with the word processor's ability to store your writing for later use or revision, means you won't have to retype the whole thing over and over again. You'll just change the parts you want to change and leave everything else the way it was and get to see it all before it's printed. Not bad, huh?

The Electronic Page

So what is this electronic page? It looks like a television screen, but it's not. In the computer world this screen is called a *cathode ray tube* (CRT) or a video display screen and is similar to the video screens at airports that tell gate numbers and flight times or the ones that are being put into department stores and libraries. When you type on a word processor, the image of the typed character, letters, numbers and special symbols (#, @, $, %, &, *, (,), +, ", :, ;) appear on the video screen. At first, it may seem strange to see what you are typing appear on a small video screen, but not for long.

Video screens, like people, come in a wide variety of sizes, shapes and color combinations. The most common is white letters on a black background, although you can get black letters on a white background (resembling an actual typewritten page) or green letters on a black background to reduce eye strain.

The Keyboard

The keys on a word processor keyboard are arranged much like a normal typewriter. Both use what's called a QWERTY keyboard. The name QWERTY comes from its mythical inventor, the eccentric Q. Qwenton Qwerty (1803-1896), who insisted that his name appear on the third row of the keyboard. In the days of the first typewriter a fast typist could easily jam the keys. Qwerty's keyboard was designed to prevent jams by slowing a typist down. So how come we still use it? Tradition.

THE WEALTHY & SOMEWHAT UNPLEASANT
Q. QUENTIN QWERTY

In addition to the normal typewriter keys, the word processor keyboard has 12 to 25 extra keys called *function keys*. The SHIFT key on a typewriter is a function key that lets us instruct the machine to print a capital letter instead of a lower-case letter. On a word processor the function keys let us tell the machine to perform all of its editing and special functions.

A plastic-covered cable connects the keyboard to the video display screen. This cable may be outside where you can see it, or inside the video screen case. Either way, it is the electronic umbilical cord connecting the keyboard to the rest of the system. This connection cable on some newer machines is flexible and on the outside, allowing you to move the keyboard around—a feature which is a real pleasure for those of us who get the wiggles after sitting in the same place typing too long. You can move the keyboard to where you will be most comfortable. By the way, the combination of a video screen and keyboard is called a *video display terminal* (or VDT).

When you press the keys on the keyboard, they respond easily to your touch with little or no pressure, like the keys on an electric typewriter. But there is a difference—no striking noise. There are no little hammers or typeballs banging against a piece of paper— just the silence of writing on an electronic page. The clicking of the

keys as your fingers press them will be the only sound you will hear. Believe it or not, Ripley, enough of us have so much trouble adjusting to that silence that some manufacturers place small speakers in the keyboard to emit a beep whenever a key is pressed. Hello, Rube Goldberg!

Some good news: If you are already a fast typist, you will be happy to hear that you'll type even faster on a good word processor because you won't be slowed down by the mechanics of printing the way you are on a typewriter.

The Computer

Nowadays computers are pretty small. They fit into some places you wouldn't expect to find them. In fact, I know a social worker who had a computer built into the handle bar of his bicycle so he could measure his speed while peddling to the unemployment office to pick up his check. In a word processing system, the computer may be either in the keyboard unit or in the video display screen case.

Actually, a computer system is really more than the physical parts of the machine: the keyboard, the CRT, and all the electrical circuits and connections. These are all hard to the touch and are called computer "hardware." There is another very important part of a computer system called "software." Software is a set of instructions that get the machine to do what you want it to do.  In the case of the word processing system, the software consists of word processing instructions (or a word processing program). The hardware could be compared to a person's physical body: bones, internal organs, eyes, blood, skin, and toenails. The software then would be the part which establishes personality and controls behavior. A major difference, or should I say one of a million major differences, between the computer and a person is that the computer can assume thousands of personalities. Just give it the Mr. Hyde program and so long Dr. Jekyll.

A computer has an electronic memory or storage area. And like people's brains, it can remember different types of things. One of the things it remembers is the computer program or software. I'll call the area of memory that the computer program is placed in the *program storage area*. I could also call it the "personality area" because it allows, actually requires, the machine to assume the personality of whatever program has been placed into this space. (Please don't go ask a salesperson about the "personality area" of the word processor. Unless they have read this book they may giggle and point.)

What we have been calling a word processor is really a small computer with a word processing program in its (personality) program storage area. It is important to realize that your word processor can become anything else you give it a program to become. If you place an accounting program or a video game program into its personality area, the system will account or play games with you. You have the power to make it become anything you want it to be. *"Vell, Dr. Frankenshtein, ve hav created a monstor."*

Besides the program storage or "personality" area, your machine's memory also has a place it can store and rearrange the material you're typing. I'll call this the *text storage work area*.

The Word Processor Program

When you purchase a word processing system you will be buying the computer hardware along with the word processing software (or program). I suggest you choose the computer program first and then purchase a machine to run the program. Programs come on what is called a "floppy" disk which looks like a 45 RPM record in its jacket. It is called floppy because you can bend it,

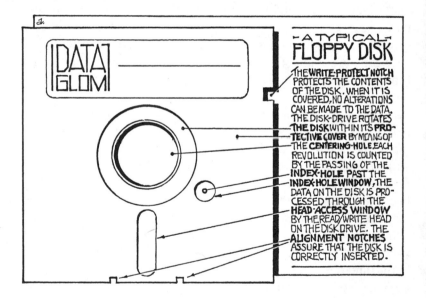

-A TYPICAL- FLOPPY DISK

THE WRITE-PROTECT NOTCH PROTECTS THE CONTENTS OF THE DISK. WHEN IT IS COVERED, NO ALTERATIONS CAN BE MADE TO THE DATA. THE DISK-DRIVE ROTATES THE DISK WITHIN ITS PROTECTIVE COVER BY MEANS OF THE CENTERING-HOLE. EACH REVOLUTION IS COUNTED BY THE PASSING OF THE INDEX-HOLE PAST THE INDEX-HOLE WINDOW, THE DATA ON THE DISK IS PROCESSED THROUGH THE HEAD-ACCESS WINDOW BY THE READ/WRITE HEAD ON THE DISK DRIVE. THE ALIGNMENT NOTCHES ASSURE THAT THE DISK IS CORRECTLY INSERTED.

although the wrapper warns you not to. The disk surface is covered with an oxide coating similar to the one used on audio and video recording tapes. It allows you to store an electronic representation of a program on its surface. The floppy disk containing the word processor program is called, appropriately enough, the *system disk* or program disk.

Alongside the video display screen are two rectangular slots with small doors on them. These are entrances to the floppy disk drives. When you insert the floppy disk into the first slot the computer can either read information from the disk, or record information onto the disk. It's a snap to tell the machine to copy the word processing program that's on the disk into its program storage area. Just open the small door, carefully slide the system disk into the slot, close the door, and press the START key. As soon as the key is pressed, the machine automatically copies into its program storage area what is on the system disk. Please note: the program is only *copied* from the disk into the memory area; the information on the disk is not erased or changed in any way! In fact it is just like playing your favorite 45 oldie.

From now on the machine is controlled by the program. A message appears on the VDT screen that says the machine is now a word processor and is ready to roll up its electronic sleeves and go to work.

Using the Word Processing Program, or, Meeting the Editor

The word processing program has the personality of an editor; it helps you correct and change the material you are typing. One of the Editor's first jobs is to set up an area in its memory to store your text. This is important, because some Editors do it better than others, as we will see later. Next, it may ask you questions such as, what day is it? who are you? and what do you want to do? Answering these questions is referred to in the trade as "signing on" to the system.

After signing on, slip a second floppy disk into the slot alongside the one where you put the system disk. It is on this second disk that you store the text you type, so let's call it the *file disk*.

After signing on and inserting your file disk for storing text, the machine just sits there waiting for you to begin typing. As you type, the keyboard electronically sends the characters you've touched to the Editor. When the Editor receives text characters it sends them to the text storage area of its memory. How can you tell what is already there or what you are putting in? You use the video display screen. It can be thought of as a window that lets you look at the electronic page (a portion of what has been put in the text storage memory). Alice, it's a looking glass of sorts that lets you see into the machine's memory.

After you've finished a writing and editing session, you may take this disk out and hide it under your mattress, or label it and put it on the shelf so later you can find your "letter of April 1 to Mr. Marvin Mudd."

Making Physical Copies of the Electronic Text

You can save the material you've typed in two ways: you can tell the word processor to print it on paper using the printer and/or to write it in electronic form on the file floppy disk that you inserted into the second disk drive. Some systems automatically store everything you have typed on the file disk as you go along. Others won't store your text onto the file disk until you tell it to do so by typing an "end edit" or "save" instruction. For these machines, a *Warning:* do not end the editing session by simply turning off the power. When you turn the power off, both the machine's program and text storage areas (the ones inside the computer itself, not the floppy disks) are erased completely, creating a sort of machine amnesia about everything you have just typed into the machine. Instead, end the editing session by typing the "end edit" or "save" instruction. Once the material is written onto a file disk the Editor can bring it back to the memory storage area at some other time to let you make additional changes and revisions.

To get a printed copy of the material you have typed, merely push one or two keys to enter the "print" command. The Editor will then organize the material and send it to the printer.

Putting It All Together

Okay ... The word processor is basically a typewriter constructed so that the keyboard is no longer attached to the print keys or the typeball. The program, which gives the computer its word processor "personality," is loaded into the computer's memory by inserting the program disk into the disk drive and pressing the start key. When you type on a word processor, the characters go into a computer instead of onto a piece of paper. You can see what you have typed by looking through the video display tube window. Material you have entered into the computer memory can be stored on the floppy file disk for later use and it can be printed on the printer whenever you are ready to put it on paper.

3
How to Operate a Word Processor: Typing and Basic Editing

In this chapter I'll tell you how to operate a typical word processor. I've arranged the material to give you a sense of the word processor personality I talked about in Chapter Two, and what it's like to work with one. If you view computers as horribly complicated machines to be avoided at all cost, or if you expect a word processor to conjure up a finished book at the press of a button, you may have to think again. This is the chapter where I'm going to help you decide if word processing is all it's cracked up to be. It's the first of four chapters on word processing software.

Start thinking "software" because most of the wonders the word processor people rave about are in the software, not the hardware.

Basic Typing and Carriage Returns

As I explained in Chapter 2, the word processor program is electronically encoded and resides on the system disk. So first you insert that disk into the system disk drive, and load the program into the machine's memory. Next you sign on to the system by inserting a file disk. Give a name to what you will be typing, and you're ready to type. When you get to the end of a line, just keep right on typing. You don't have to press a carriage return key. When a word reaches the

right-hand margin, the next character entered causes the entire word to move to the beginning of the next line. This nifty feature is known in the trade as a *wordwrap* or *automatic return*. If you're a super typist, you may find this feature a little difficult to adjust to at first. But you'll soon get used to it. As a matter of fact you will probably wonder how you ever lived without it. You'll be typing much faster (more words per minute) because you can type with a constant rhythm, never having to slow down at the end of a line to return the carriage or type ball while figuring out if a word will fit on a line. By the way, the word processor does not have a MARGIN RELEASE key. There is no need for one. The RETURN key on the word processor keyboard is used only when you want the next character you type to start a new line. You would use this key to begin a new paragraph, type a title line, or table of numbers, etc.

Moving Around the Page

On a typewriter there is a pointer just below the carriage that shows your place on the line. The word processor marks your place

THE CURSOR

this is the very false gallop of verse

on the video screen with a small square of light known as a *cursor*. The cursor doesn't shout out foul language; it just shows you where the next typed character will be placed. As you type, the cursor moves merrily along the line lighting the way across the screen.

You can position the cursor anywhere on the screen by using the four keyboard keys with arrows on them. Pressing one of these directional keys moves the cursor one position in the direction of the arrow. Moving the cursor doesn't change any of the characters on the screen, it just lights up the position it's on, whether there is a character there or not. But watch out! If you type while the cursor is

DIRECTIONALS

positioned over a character, that character will be replaced by whatever you type. This feature lets you operate the word processor as if it were a correcting typewriter. Just back up and type over the part you want to change.

While I'm at it, let me mention spacing out. If you forget you're not using a typewriter and try to move the cursor by using the space bar, rather than the directional keys, you will find that blank spaces will be placed where you once had characters and words. So be prepared for some accidental erasing while adjusting to this difference between the typewriter and the word processor. (And kindly do not become a cursor yourself; you'll get used to it.)

Scrolling

The typical video screen lets you look at only 24 lines of your text at one time. So if you are typing something longer, how do you review material that exceeds 24 lines? Well, remember how the screen is only a window looking into the memory? Since memory is

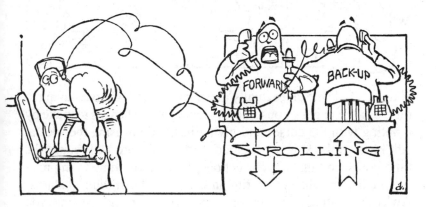

like a large scroll, you can work on as much material as will fit on the scroll (the available text memory area), and that's a lot more than 24 lines.

On the keyboard are two scrolling keys, one labeled ADVANCE and the other BACKUP. Pressing either of these keys informs the Editor that you want to move a different segment of the text into the viewing window. The scroll keys direct the scroll to move up or down one line at a time. If you want to see either the previous page or the following page, press the PAGE key before pressing the scroll key. This lets you skim through the text a screen page at a time, moving the text faster than the credits of a movie with a cast of thousands.

Editing

The editing features of the word processor are the unfulfilled dream of anyone using a standard typewriter. These features enable

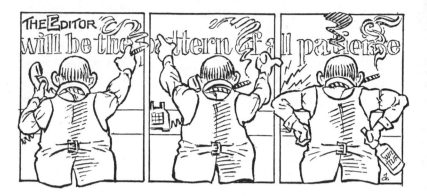

you to add, delete and actually move text around without having to retype entire pages. You tell the machine what changes to make by pointing with the cursor and giving instructions using the special edit keys on the keyboard. Good editing software will reduce the time you spend making corrections, leaving you time to improve the quality of what you write and fill your heart with gladness. Awkward editing software may slow you down and frustrate you no end. So, when you shop around for a word processing system, pay a whole lot of attention to how many keystrokes it takes for each of the editing functions and how complicated it is to do routine editing jobs. And before going shopping, read Chapter 11 on selecting a word processor.

Editing: Inserting New Material into the Text

The process of adding additional characters, words, sentences, or even pages into the text is called *inserting* and here's how to do it. Move the cursor to the postion where you want to insert the new material. Press the INSERT key and the line the cursor is on will split apart, like the Red Sea, leaving space to type in the new material. In most systems the new material you are typing is displayed on the screen in what is called *highlight mode*, distinguishing it from the rest of the text. As you continue to insert, the remainder of the old text moves down the screen leaving space for the new words. While you are typing the new material you still have the opportunity to type over mistakes to make corrections. When you're finished inserting, just press the ENTER key and presto!—the text closes up and the highlighting disappears, leaving the new material looking as if it had been there from the very beginning.

But, let's say that before you've pressed the ENTER key you change your mind about inserting what you've just typed, then you press the CLEAR key and the highlighted material disappears leaving everything exactly as it was before you pressed the insert key. Simple isn't it?

Editing: Deleting Material

Deleting erases material from the text, then closes up the space that's left. To delete, position the cursor over the first character to be deleted and press the DELETE key. This highlights that character. If you want to delete more than a single

character, tell the Editor how much more by pressing either the WORD, SENTENCE, PARAGRAPH, or PAGE keys. The act of pressing the DELETE key sequence (word, sentence, etc.) does not cause material to be deleted, just highlights it. Nothing is actually deleted until you press the ENTER key. Pressing the ENTER key causes all of the highlighted text to disappear and the remaining text to close up as if the deleted material had never existed. If you change your mind about deleting the highlighted material, pressing the CLEAR key will take you out of delete mode, turn off the highlighting, and leave your original material as is.

You may end up moaning and tearing your hair out if you accidentally press the ENTER key when you meant to press the CLEAR key. Relax, this is part of the fun of you and your word processor getting to know each other. And of course, you can always retype material using the insert feature.

Editing: Cut and Paste

To "cut and paste" is the old-fashioned way of moving a section of text from one place in a manuscript to another. The word processor Editor can do it easily once you show it the text you want to move. You mark the beginning by moving the cursor to the first character of the block of text to be moved and press the BLOCK START key. Then move the cursor to the last character in the block and press BLOCK END to mark the end of the block. The Editor then highlights all of the material between the two block markers to show you what it will be moving.

If you've goofed, just reenter the block start or block end at the correct position. When the correct segment of text is highlighted on the screen, move the cursor to where you want it to go and press the MOVE key. Presto Changeo! The material is electronically cut from its original postion and pasted in where you told the Editor you wanted it. If your word processing software enables you to do this efficiently, that is, without annoying delays or a complicated series of keystrokes—it's worth its weight in typewriter ribbons.

Editing: Text Searching

Picture yourself sitting at your word processor with 50 pages of a manuscript you are revising for the umpteenth time, with several corrections still to be made. You don't feel like tediously scrolling along a line or even a page at a time to get the part that needs changing to appear on the video display screen. So what do you do? You use the *search mode*.

The search mode enables you to find a word, a phrase or any grouping of characters in the text. For example, suppose I wanted to find this section beginning at the words "Text Searching." First I position the cursor at the beginning of the text (most systems only allow you to search forward in this mode. A rare few will let you search forward or backward through the text.). Then, I press the search key and type "Text Search" or perhaps "Text Sea" for short. I press the ENTER key and the Editor goes searching through the complete text storage area. When it finds the right group of characters—or *text string* as it is called—it places the cursor at that location in the text.

The trick to using the search mode is to specify the exact text string you want, otherwise you may get some unexpected results.

For instance, if you start a search for the string "*be*," the system will not only find "*be*" but "*be*en" "com*be*d" and even "*be*lch, excuse me." You can avoid this problem by simply defining the string as (space) "*be*" (space) or (*be*). But until you get accustomed to defining strings precisely, you'll be amused at the things that will unexpectedly turn up in a text search.

Editing: Search and Replace

This is not the name of a new Special Forces tactic to fight a guerilla war. The Search and Replace mode lets you find a specified character string and automatically replace it with another. With one command I could change every occurrence of the word "program" in this book to the words "machine personality" or even to "rutabaga." This is incredibly useful. If, for instance, you have consistently made a spelling error, one fell swoop and it's all corrected. In the search and replace mode you can instruct the Editor to stop at each occurrence of a text string to let you decide whether you want to make the change, or you can tell the Editor to make all the changes automatically, which is called a *global change*.

I am a lousy typist. Therefore when I wrote this book, I used the search and replace mode to avoid typing certain long words. Every time I wanted to write "word processor" I typed "wp." Then at the end of each section, I had the Editor do a global change automatically changing every occurrence of "wp" to "word processor."

The only shortcoming I find in this feature is that if you are changing something in a long document, it may take several minutes to complete. This can be a little frustrating if you are impatient to get on with the editing. Just think about how much time it would take to do it longhand and go get a glass of juice or a cup of coffee.

Editing: Combined Operations

Most editing requires using a series of editing commands to delete, insert, and move portions of the text. Combining the editing commands enables you to make any changes you could want to a

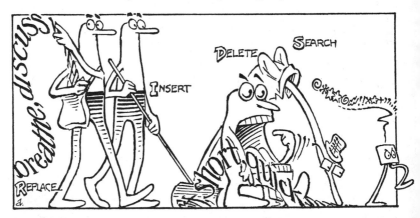

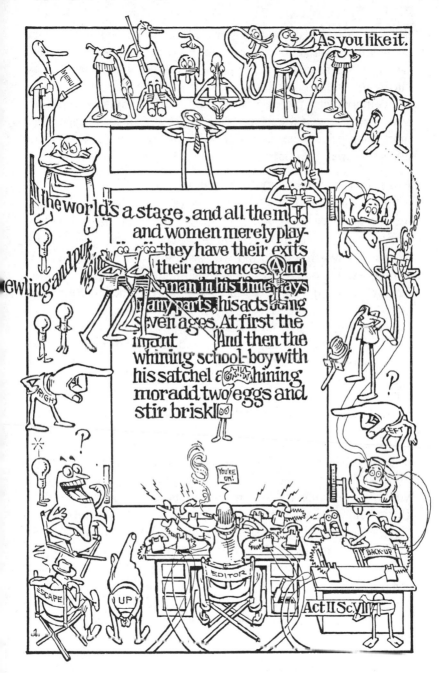

body of written material. For some editing you probably won't use any editing commands at all because for certain types of revisions it is simpler and faster to just retype that portion of the text. Once you get into it, you will discover your own way to make the editing zip along.

In emergencies there is always the ESCAPE key which will stop any operation you might have initiated by mistake. Escape could more appropriately be called the "whoops" or "undo" key because it lets you change your mind without creating a mess to clean up.

Editing: Tab Setting and Margins

Just below the control line at the top of the screen is a ruler that's used to indicate the settings for the left and right margins and the tabs. You guessed it—"L" for left and "R" for right. See the figure; it's worth a thousand words. In contrast to the typewriter which has only one type of tab setting, the word processor has two. The tabs can align the text you are typing along the left column, or on a decimal point. Why a decimal point, you say? Ever try entering a column of numbers on a typewriter? It takes a lot of counting and backspacing to get everything to line up.

Setting the tabs is easy. Just position the cursor at the place you want the tab to be set and press the TABSET key, followed by either a "T" or a dot, and it's set. To clear, press the CONTROL key followed by a "C" and that tab or margin will be cleared.

Editing: The Way It Really Is

I don't want to give you an oversimplified view of what editing is all about. There is an incredible difference between the time it takes you to start editing and the time it takes to feel comfortable editing. Basic editing may be learned in about an hour, while feeling comfortable about using a system can take as long as a week. Some people never really get to feel comfortable with the advanced commands. So, start simple and get into it at your own pace. Learn each option when you are ready for it. Expand your horizons when what you are doing requires it or when you are just plain ready to move on.

And remember, before purchasing any system, look closely at the training manual that comes with the machine. Next to taking the salesperson home, it will be your biggest helper. If the training material on the system is as clear as mud, do not buy the machine!

Good editing software will reduce the time you spend making corrections, leaving you more time to improve the quality of what you write. Awkward editing software may slow you down and possibly frustrate you no end. So, when you shop around for your word processing system, pay a whole lot of attention to how many keystrokes it takes for each of the editing functions and how complicated it is to do the routine editing jobs.

So . . . typing on a word processor is not all that different from typing on a typewriter. It does have some nifty features (such as the automatic carriage return) that let you type faster while making typing more enjoyable. Special keys and a cursor (@#$%¢!) enable you to insert, delete, and move parts of the text. This means you may never have to type entire pages over again to correct mistakes. As a matter of fact, with a word processor, correcting mistakes becomes almost as easy as making them.

4
Formatting: Text Layout and Printing

Want to be able to type that technical report or resume only once and with the touch of a few keys change how it will look when it is printed? Well, the word processor can *format* (that is, arrange) your material in as many ways as you can imagine, without your having to do anything more than give it a short series of commands. You can tell it how wide to make the margins, how to space the lines, and how much to indent the paragraphs. Let's say you've done all that and still don't like how it looks. So change your mind and change the margin width, line spacing and paragraph indentations, and the system automatically adjusts the text to fit your new format. It'll even number or, in this case, re-number the pages. Sounds incredible, doesn't it? And, once you set the print formatting, you don't have to mess with it again until you want to change it. For example, you can print double-spaced copy which leaves room for making corrections. Then, after you enter the corrections, by simply changing a format command you can print the text in the final single-spaced form.

Text Layout

When I talk about text layout I mean all the details that determine how text will look printed on paper. Now, if you don't want to spend the time to design it yourself, the word processor will do it for you, using standard settings called *default values*. When you're

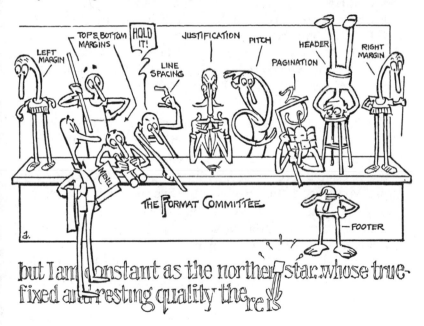

first learning to operate a word processor, using the default values permits you to type and edit without worrying about setting up text layout or format commands. You may want to use this form of automatic pilot until you encounter special circumstances that force a change. My friend, Carol, who is helping edit this book, has worked on several word processors and managed to never learn the formatting commands. She's also never learned how to spell rutabaga. You learn only what you need to for the jobs you're working on.

Setting the Format

So how do you set the format you've selected from the options that your system offers? On the keyboard is a special function key labeled FORMAT. When you press it, the text on the screen disappears (but is not erased) and what's known as a *format menu* appears in its place. The format menu displays *default values* (pre-set parameters) that you can change to suit your needs.

```
Print Format
Document: CHAPTER 4      Pages: 12
LM-Left Margin    10     J-Justify          L
RM-Right Margin   75     P-Pitch           10
TM-Top Margin      6     PN-Page Number     1
BM-Bottom Margin   6     PI-Para Indent     5
LS-Line Space      1     PS-Para Space      1
NL-Number Lines   66
```

To change any of the format specifications listed above, type its abbreviated name (NL, J, PI), then an equal sign and the setting you want it to have. For example, to change the line spacing from single to double space, type LS=2, then press the RETURN key. Voila, you'll see on the menu that the line spacing is now set to 2. You may change any of the format values as often as you like. When you change the print format you do so only for the portion of text that follows your new command.

Let's clarify this with an example. Say you wanted to indent only a portion of something you are typing. Move the cursor to the first character of that section and hit (gently) the FORMAT key. The format menu will appear to let you enter the new value for the margin. Next press the RETURN key and text will appear with the new margin. Move the cursor to the end of the indented section, recall the format menu, and restore the margins to their original setting by another command.

Setting the Margins

Margins define the boundaries of the print on a page. Let's say that we want a one-inch space on both sides of our printed page. For a printer that prints 80 characters across the width of a standard piece of paper (8½x11), a one-inch left margin starts at position 10, and a one-inch right margin starts at position 70. To set these margins press the format key to order the format menu, then type in LM=10 for the left margin and RM=70 for the right. So much for the sides. You set the top margin by telling the editor how many blank lines to skip at the top of each page. The bottom margin? You guessed it. You tell it how many lines to leave blank at the bottom of every page. A standard piece of paper holds 66 lines and a typical top and bottom margin would be 6 lines each. The more sophisticated systems specify the margin in inches rather than characters or lines. But you set them in the same way.

Justification

This doesn't mean an acceptable excuse for taking a two-week lunch hour. On a typewriter the print is usually flush (or straight) along the left margin and uneven (or ragged) on the right margin. This margin *justification* is called *flush left* or *ragged right*. On a word processor, you can turn the tables and print flush right and ragged left. This can also be used for placing headings or page numbers on the right side of pages.

You can also set it so both the left and right margins are flush, and that's called *text justified*. This book is text justified. The word processing system creates even margins by placing spaces between the words to make all the lines the same length. The spaces are distributed across the line as evenly as possible; and some systems do it better than others. For example, a low-cost printer, can only insert full character spaces between the words. Even if the extra spaces are distributed across the line, this can look terrible, just like this   line.   On   the   other   hand,   a   precision   letter quality printer will equally distribute the spacing. It uses partial spaces between all the words, giving the lines a more consistent appearance, like the lines in this book. Some word processing systems can make a precision letter quality printer do *space justified printing*, sometimes called letterspacing. In addition to placing the extra line spacing between words, small spaces are also inserted between the characters to spread out the letters in the words. The resulting text has a completely even appearance, but some words may be given a bit of emphasis unintentionally.

The last of the justifications—as if we needed another one—is text centered and in this mode each line of text is centered between the margins—a must for title pages.

Text Entered Commands, or, I Come Here Often

When I am first learning to operate a word processing system, calling up the format menu saves me from memorizing all the formatting commands and codes when there is so much else to remember. But once I become a "real pro" on the word processor, using the menus becomes a nuisance. After all, if you eat at the same restaurant every night you wouldn't have to see a menu. You'd just order.

Once you learn the ropes, the easy way to format is to place your format order directly while you're editing by using an *imbedded command line*. This line starts with a special character like an *. When the Editor sees an asterisk as the first character on a line, it knows that what follows is a format order. Smart fellow that it is, it uses the information on that line to change the format menu values. So, if in the middle of typing text you enter the following line:

*LS=2, J=L RETURN

the Editor sets the format for double spacing and reshapes the text you're about to type so it's left justified. It leaves it that way until you make another change.

Numbering Pages

Although a word processor will not write your book for you, it will automatically number your pages. If you want to start with a number other than 1, tell it the number you want by using the format menu or an imbedded command. Page numbers appear on the format menu as PN. Most systems will display the page breaks and numbers as a part of the text. The automatic paging feature lets you insert and delete material without worrying about renumbering pages. It will adjust its numbers to account for changes you've made to the material. Well, what if you don't want the page to end where the automatic pager wants it? An override function is included so you can start a new page anytime you want one.

There are two types of word processing systems: those that let you view the text as it will actually be printed and those that don't. If you can't view the text in final form, there is a good chance that the printout will contain what are known as *widows* and *orphans*. An 'orphan' is a title line or the first line of a paragraph that is left as the last line on a page. A 'widow' is the last line fragment of a section that appears as the first line of a new page. If you have an inhumane word processor that doesn't take care of widows and orphans by decreasing or extending the number of lines on a page, printing can become a real pain. You have to first print your document to see where the page breaks are. Then you reset the page breaks to remove the widows and orphans and reprint only to find new ones. Sound horrible? It is! The moral: purchase a humane word processor that automatically takes care of orphans and widows.

Headers and Footers

A header is information you place at the top of each page. You see the headers at the top of the pages of this book. Likewise, a footer is information printed at the bottom of each page. For instance, the page numbers in many books are placed on the bottom right and left sides of the odd and even pages. Your word processor can do the same. You may enter the header and footer text through the menu or by means of an imbedded command. Headers and footers can be changed at any point in the text or suppressed, as on a title page. You just override the command at that point in the text by entering the header or footer as a blank line. Yep, if it's blank it can't be printed.

Special Print Functions

Special keyboard sequences let you enter commands to underline portions of the text. Usually this command is performed by sending a character to the printer followed by a backspace and underline character. The overall effect of the print sequence is to print the character, then backspace and finally print the underline. As a matter of fact, the Editor handles this in the same way that you would on a typewriter. Commands for overstriking (make a character appear darker) or boldfacing (overprints the characters with the character slightly offset) are also handled by backspacing and overprinting. Commands for subscripts (like the 2 in H_2O) and superscripts (like the 2 in 16^2), requiring the page to be rolled forward or backward a half line, are also imbedded in the text as a printer control command.

Pitch, the character size of the print element (or type face), is entered in the body of the text or from the menu. The pitch refers to the number of characters per inch that will be printed on a line. Common word processor pitch elements are:

Pica (10 pitch): 10 characters per inch
Elite (12 pitch): 12 characters per inch
Micron (15 pitch): 15 characters per inch
Proportional Print: The number of characters per inch varies because, like people, some characters are fatter than others. An "N" is twice the width of an "i".

Not all word processors will allow the choice of all four types of print elements. If you will be using different print sizes in your writing make sure your word processor will support the function and that the printer you're using is capable of using different print sizes.

Please note that the display screen on all word processing systems, except those used by the newspaper and publishing industry, display all textual material in a fixed-size character. This means that boldfaced print, subscripting and character sizes are indicated on the screen by *reverse video* (reversing the text and background colors for emphasis) or underlining. Various manufacturers have different ways of indicating the special print functions. Most systems have a function key that will alter the text display to make code characters invisible. In this way you can see how the text layout looks without the coded symbols that were used to create the layout.

Printing

You can print a document from its storage location on a floppy disk, or from memory if you are in the midst of editing it. Enter the format menu by pressing the FORMAT key. Then type PRINT and the complete document you are typing will be printed. To print from the current cursor position to the end of the text, type PRINT E. To print a stored document on a floppy disk while you are editing something else, enter the format screen and type PRINT, followed by the stored document's name. The printer will start and you can continue editing while it is printing.

Putting It All Together

Formatting is giving your word processor all the layout details for how you want your material to look when it is printed. These details may be entered through the format menu or by using imbedded commands. The instruction to print a segment of text is given by typing PRINT from the format menu. Beware! Working with and using the format commands is the most difficult part of word processing. Go slow learning these procedures and be prepared to run through a lot of paper while learning.

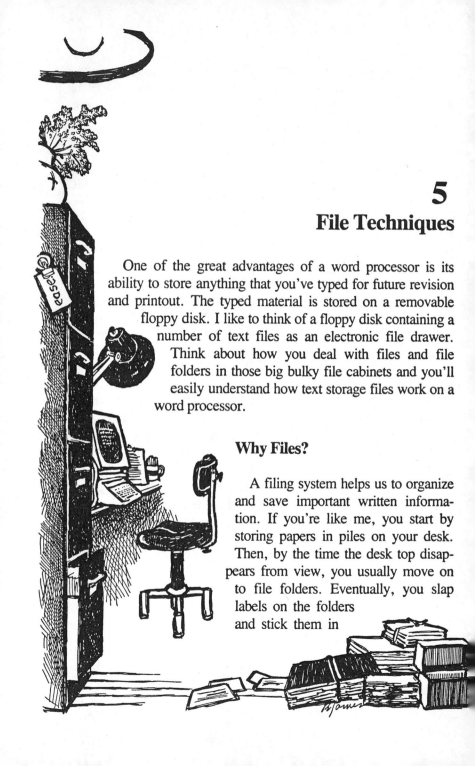

5
File Techniques

One of the great advantages of a word processor is its ability to store anything that you've typed for future revision and printout. The typed material is stored on a removable floppy disk. I like to think of a floppy disk containing a number of text files as an electronic file drawer. Think about how you deal with files and file folders in those big bulky file cabinets and you'll easily understand how text storage files work on a word processor.

Why Files?

A filing system helps us to organize and save important written information. If you're like me, you start by storing papers in piles on your desk. Then, by the time the desk top disappears from view, you usually move on to file folders. Eventually, you slap labels on the folders and stick them in a file cabinet drawer. I usually put my most important papers, like the notes and reference material for this book, to say nothing of the lucrative contract from my publisher, in the top drawer. My bottom drawer is full of former lives; things I just refuse to throw out such as old love letters and income tax forms from 20 years ago. You just never know.

You organize electronic files on a floppy disk just as you'd organize files in a drawer. A disk the size of a 45 rpm record will store anywhere from 50 to 500 pages of typed material. Now that's a nice size file drawer! The pros call each floppy file drawer a *storage volume*, but I'll stick with file drawer for now. Within this electronic file drawer are a series of individual files or documents. The term *document*, by the way, is what all the word processor manuals call anything you type. Great, we can store poem documents and recipe documents and book documents and even document documents. So, when I say document, think of whatever you may be writing and storing on your word processor.

Setting Up the Electronic File Drawer

How do you prepare the floppy disk for use as a file drawer? Start by entering the *disk format command* to the word processing system. Disk formatting is *not* the same as text formatting. The disk format command will initiate a series of instructions that will take you step by step through the disk formatting process.

The first thing the Formatter asks for is the name of the disk. Naming a disk is like labeling the file drawer. So you type in a name like "top drawer," "my file," or "A-J," and lo and behold, it's named.

On the better systems, the disk formatter will ask if you want to attach any descriptive notes to the floppy disk to remind you what's stored where. Because I always assume I'll remember what I put on a disk, I never make meticulous notes. Inevitably I find myself pulling my hair out while searching through a pile of floppys trying to figure out what I've put where. So, beware, always use the space the system provides for you for descriptive notes. You will save yourself and your scalp a lot of grief. I now have so many floppys that I purchased a special catalog program to just let me keep track of what is where.

Next, the Formatter asks for a *code word*. The code word is like a lock for the file drawer. Now look around and be sure no one is looking over your shoulder. Coast clear? Good. Type in your code

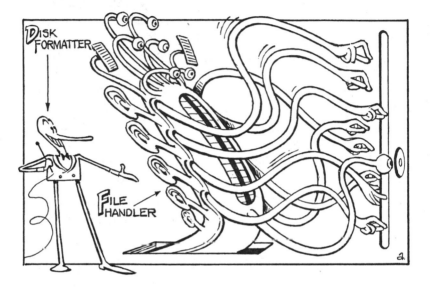

word. If you don't want to lock your electronic file drawer, just say, "never mind" by pressing RETURN.

The Formatter immediately starts writing control information to your disk to get it ready for use. It's a little like using a machine to draw lines on a piece of paper you'll be writing on. A good Formatter will not only prepare the disk (draw the lines) but will check to make sure the entire disk is suitable for writing on. If it finds trouble spots it will automatically "lock out" these sections so the Editor will not attempt to put any of your text there.

Folders for the File Cabinet

Let's see, so far we have a file drawer named "top drawer" which may or may not have a lock on it. So now let's put some file folders in it. The word processing system automatically labels electronic file folders when you tell it you want to type a new document. Before it allows you to begin typing, it asks you to type in the document name—that's the label. So first you label the file folder, then you begin writing what goes in it. This is totally the reverse of the way you do it by typewriter where you write something first and set up the folder afterward.

Each system has its own rules for naming the document file folder. The worst system I've seen restricts you to an eight-character name; the best allows an 80-character name for the document and additional space to enter descriptive notes. But the one rule common to all systems is "only one document for each file folder."

Effective naming of files requires creative thinking. You want a name that is unique and descriptive enough to help you recall what's in the document later. A name like LETTER is OK if you've written only one. A better one might be LREAGAN1/14 standing for "the letter to Ronald Reagan on Jan 14." Your other love letters could be labeled similarly. However, if you have only 8 characters to use for a file name, it will take ingenuity to make your files unique and memorable. For instance, LRR1/14.

Filing the Folders

Once your document has a file name, the system sets up a space on the disk for that file. When you hit the SAVE key, that file will be stored in that space. It's a good idea to save your text every so often while you're typing rather than waiting till the end. That way if your system fails in mid-stream you won't lose the whole thing. Conversely, if you want to delete files from the disk when you no longer need them, just press the DELETE FILE key, then enter the file name. This is analogous to removing a file folder from the file drawer and throwing it in the fire.

Here's how I set up the disks and files for this book. The text is stored on four floppy disks. These disks are named: "WP Chap1-6," "WP Chap7-12," "WP Chap12-16," and "WP Gloss&App." The files on the "WP Chap12-16" disk are named: "Chapt12," "Chapt13," "Chapt14A," and "Chapt14B." While I was editing the rough copy, I set up a separate file for each version of each chapter. Then, when I completed the final version of a chapter, I deleted the obsolete versions from the disk. Are you wondering why I stored Chapter 12 on two files? Well, it was a very long chapter. I split it up to speed the process of copying it into and out of memory, which I had to do every time I worked with it. Segmenting a file in this way is called, believe it or not, *file segmenting*. Segmented files may be put back together when it's time to print them out.

Backing Up Your Files

Most word processors have a *file backup* feature which automatically makes a copy of your files each time you edit them. Let's say I tell my system that I want to edit Chapter 4. The word processor program will copy the file named Chapt4 to a work file (on the same disk). When I finish editing and issue a "save command," the program replaces the original Chapt4 with the edited Chapt4, and places the original Chapt4 in a file named *Chapt4.bak*. Now I have two distinct versions of the same chapter on the same disk. So, if I change my mind and want the original version for some reason, I can easily get it.

The automatic backup feature will protect your work from power failures and errors made in writing to the disk. But it doesn't offer protection from someone sitting on or spilling coffee on your disk, which will destroy everything including both the original and the backup. The backup feature does have the disadvantage of using up disk space rapidly, and to back up the latest version of the file, you must save it on still another disk. But, on balance, it's worth it.

When a disk fails it is like having everything in your file drawer self-destruct. Goodbye file information, I'll never see you again! Unless I can remember and am able to retype you. In the computer world, your insurance is duplication. So how do you protect yourself and your files from coffee spillers, disk sitters and other disk destroyers? Some computer projects are so critical they not only require duplicate files and disks but duplicate computers as well to insure against failure. So, make it a point to copy all of your important files to another disk. With a single command, usually called *disk backup* (not to be confused with the just-mentioned file backup command), your word processor automatically copies all the material from one disk onto another.

Backing up disks is easy. What's hard is remembering to do it!

File Storage Formats

Files are stored on a disk in one of three formats:

1) Text storage format
2) Print format
3) Data processing format

Here's what this means:

The *text storage format* is the most common way word processors store what people have typed. Only text stored in this manner can be called up to the screen for editing. The file already contains the formatting commands needed for printing (you put them in when you set up that file). When it's time to print text stored in this format, the word processing program reads the text file, interprets the formatting commands, and then sets up the print lines accordingly. The word processing program then sends each line to the printer for printing.

Each word processor uses its own text storage format, so the files from one word processor cannot be read by another without a conversion program.

When you store text in *print format*, the lines of text on the disk look exactly as they will look when printed. In other words, the program interprets the formatting commands before it stores the text on disk. This format is used on word processors that can edit and print simultaneously. Text stored in print format can go directly from the disk to the printer without going through the word processing program. This allows the program to edit another file at the same time the sytem is printing. This format is also used to store text that must await the availability of a busy printer, as is often the case when more than one word processor is sharing a single printer. "OK, File #4, you're now third in line for the printer. Don't call us, we'll call you when we're ready."

As a last resort, *print format files* can always be transferred between different word processors. The only thing required to edit them in the new system is a series of search and replace commands to remove all of the printer controls. I've used this in a pinch and it works.

The *data processing format* stores your material in a form that can be handled easily by non-word processor programs. A customer name and address file, for example, would be stored in this format to be used in a list processing operation. This is primarily used by programmers to enter program text, or data for use by other programs.

The Care and Handling of Floppy Disks

A floppy disk always lives inside a protective cardboard cover, like a turtle in its shell. Never remove a disk from its protective cover, even when you insert it into a disk drive where a small movable electronic gizmo reads from it and writes information to it. When not in use, keep the disk in the paper envelope it came in and store it in an upright position. Just like a turtle.

If you want a disk to live a long and useful life, do not touch the exposed disk surface. The skin surface liquids on your fingers can cause disk read-and-write problems. You don't have to worry about cleaning floppys; the inside of their jackets contains a felt type material that removes dirt and dust from the disk surface as it spins around. When labeling a disk be sure to use a felt tip pen, instead of a ball point, to avoid damaging its delicate surface. Also, avoid leaving the disk in direct sunlight where it could melt. The safe temperature range for floppys is 50-125° Farenheit.

Beware of magnets! All the information you've typed, edited and stored on a floppy disk is encoded as magnetic charges on the disk surface . . . so a magnet placed close to a disk could really screw things up. I once had a major portion of a disk become unreadable because it was placed on a magnetized screwdriver. I now know why they're called screwdrivers. I always hear stories about magnetized paper clips doing the same thing. The strangest one I ever heard was of a phone inadvertently placed on a disk, which wiped it out when the bell rang. Phones use an electromagnet to ring the bell. Hmmm . . . I think I'll try it out.

DON'T PLAY GAMES W/ FLOPPIES

I've got some good news. I just touched a disk to a phone surface while it was ringing and nothing happened to it. Seems like that one is just one more of those watch-out theoretical computer rumors that everyone talks about, but no one ever checks. You'd like to know how I checked the disk after the phone rang? I used the *disk verification portion* of my system's format program to see if everything was O.K., and it was.

Many manuals advise removing disks from the disk drives before turning the power on or off. I never remember to remove them. As a matter of fact I don't even try anymore; I just leave disks in all the time. Try it on your machine with a disk that is not vital. Few of the newer machines will affect your disks unless you turn the power off while information is being written to or read from the disk. And why would anybody every do that? Well, if you're like me, and believe in Murphy's law, you'll do it at least once while writing information on the most critical disk you own and then find your backup disk is lost.

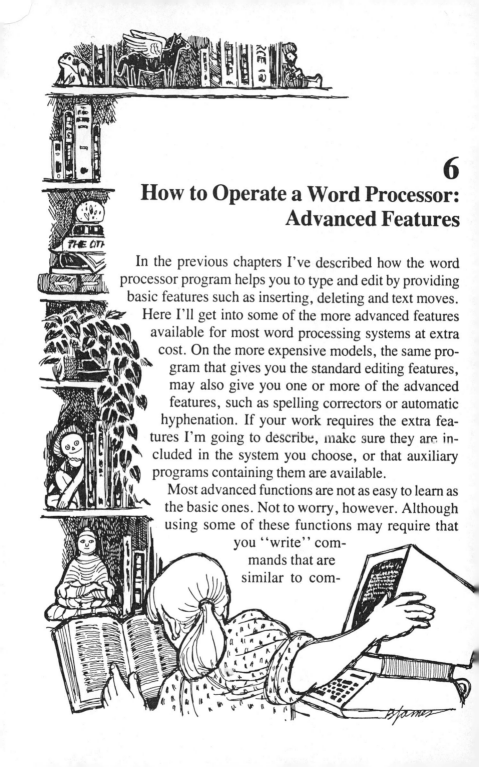

6
How to Operate a Word Processor: Advanced Features

In the previous chapters I've described how the word processor program helps you to type and edit by providing basic features such as inserting, deleting and text moves. Here I'll get into some of the more advanced features available for most word processing systems at extra cost. On the more expensive models, the same program that gives you the standard editing features, may also give you one or more of the advanced features, such as spelling correctors or automatic hyphenation. If your work requires the extra features I'm going to describe, make sure they are included in the system you choose, or that auxiliary programs containing them are available.

Most advanced functions are not as easy to learn as the basic ones. Not to worry, however. Although using some of these functions may require that you "write" commands that are similar to computer programming instructions, you don't have to be a genius to learn them.

Even if you don't have the time or inclination to use the advanced features, find out what they are. They can help your typing or editing productivity. On the other hand, just because you purchase a word processor with lots of advanced features doesn't mean you'll ever use them. Which brings me to another point: it's smart to take whatever training your word processor salespeople offer. Otherwise, you may never know the machine's possibilities. If someone other than you will be doing the typing, send him or her to classes too; don't expect anyone to magically learn the advanced features.

Dictionaries or Spelling Correctors

If, like me, you were always among the first kids knocked out of your school's spelling bees on a word like *rutabaga*, you'll be happy to know there are dictionary programs available for use with your word processor. If you're typing and come to a word that you can't spell, use the dictionary's look-up function control key to check your spelling. In addition to checking individual words these programs will automatically check your entire manuscript, or portions of it, for spelling errors, by comparing each word you've typed against its own vocabulary list—usually from 20,000 to 100,000 words long. If a word turns up that is not in the dictionary, it'll be highlighted and you must decide if that word needs to be corrected. To help you decide, the program may show you the words in its vocabulary which are closest to the spelling of the word in question. If the word is misspelled, just tell the program the correct spelling and it'll make the correction.

A good dictionary program allows you to add words to its vocabulary. That's a great feature for a technical writer because technical terms are not a standard part of dictionary vocabularies. Most dictionary programs allow you to enter up to 10,000 of your own words. Now here's the bad news. While a dictionary program will highlight words that don't match any words in its vocabulary, it won't pick up mistakes in word usage. For example, if you said "I wood" instead of "I would," or "what an enormous feet" instead of "what an enormous feat," it wouldn't spot these errors because all of the words used are part of its vocabulary. The dictionary program, then, is most useful for finding typos, such as places where a space between words was inadvertently omitted, and misspellings which create collections of letters that aren't recognized words. In other "woids," it will not replace proofreading.

In addition to dictionary programs that are used while you're typing and editing, there's a class of programs called *spelling checkers* that are run on their own to check text files stored on a disk for spelling errors. The better of these programs will not only display the unrecognized words it has found, but will let you view each of them along with the rest of the sentence they are in. This technique, called *viewing in context*, helps you to figure out spelling errors and typos that make no sense. As each word is shown you can correct, skip over it or enter it into the dictionary. When you've gone through all the words, the program chugs off and automatically makes all the corrections you requested. The real cheapie spelling checkers will not correct the spelling errors but only mark them in the text file with a character like a #. You then have to re-edit the file using the search function to make the corrections.

Since I am a poor speller, I prefer a dictionary program I can use while I am actually writing. Why purchase a spelling checker rather than a dictionary program? You got it: the price. Dictionary programs cost about $200, spelling checkers about $50-$75.

Other Writing Helpers

I recently purchased a thesaurus program. So now, while writing, I can place the cursor at the beginning of any word, press a control key and have a whole list of possible replacement words displayed on the screen. Press a second key and the original word is replaced by an alternate.

There are also word counters and grammar checkers, none of which I find too valuable. I even tried a program that points out the use of sexist terms in your writing. When it said that I should change "mention" to a nonsexist term, I gave up using it. I *"persontion"* this only to advise you to try out any program before purchase.

Indexing Routines

If you've ever written a book or manual and had to index it you'll be relieved to know that this tedious and time-consuming task has been automated. Indexing programs scan an entire document to either locate commonly used words and phrases in the text or to locate words and phrases which you've told it to look for. All you professional indexers out there will be happy to know that indexing routines will not replace manual indexing because things like cross-referencing will still have to be done by hand. But they make the tedious parts a lot easier, at least.

Indexing programs include both manual and automatic entry of words to appear in the index. The automated programs read your text files and display all candidate words for indexing. When you have indicated all the words you want in the index the program automatically compiles, alphabetizes and creates the index listing.

Print It and You're Finished

I prefer the manual indexing systems that let you mark either words or text sections you want to appear in the index. The mark is a special symbol that displays on the screen where you can see it but never appears in your printed text. After your entire manuscript has been marked, run the index program in what is called *batch mode* The indexer will collect the marked sections from a batch of files or chapters. To do this you must list the sections or chapters to be linked together unless you have the entire manuscript stored as a single file. The starting page number on each file must be manually set to the number the preceding one ended with. Once again, the result of the program is an alphabetized index to your book.

What do you do if you want to index a book you have typed and edited on your word processor but which is being printed by a phototypesetter? The normal procedure would be to send your word processor text files to the phototypesetter over the telephone (see Chapter 15). The typesetter will readjust your formatting to make the final layout. This means that the page breaks in your files no longer correspond to the page breaks of the actual book. Dilemma of dilemmas! My suggestion is: never create an index for anything unless it is in final print form. Enter the special markings, but don't create the index. When the typesetter sends back the final galley proofs of the book containing the actual page numbers, then it's time to start creating the index.

To get correct page numbers, go through your text files and create page breaks exactly where they are in the galley sheets. To insure that the system doesn't enter page breaks of its own, you may have to increase the text margin by as much as fifty percent. This is done because the galleys are proportionally printed and will contain more characters on each line than your text files. The only page breaks in the manuscript must be the ones you enter manually. Your files will probably look absurd, but don't worry about it. The files now have page numbers corresponding to the galleys, so it's time to run the indexing program. Presto, before you can say Q. Qwenton Qwerty, the final index is complete with the actual page numbers. Set up your machine's communication link, dial the typesetter's number, send the index file and the table of contents, and your book is ready for printing. Almost.

Hyphenation

For aesthetic reasons you may want to hyphenate overly long words instead of letting the Editor move the entire word to the next line. It's easy to do with a hyphenation feature which is standard in most word processing software.

Here's how you use it. The Editor defines what is called a *hot zone*—a series of characters at the end of each line which contain words that are hyphenation candidates. It's like the bell on a typewriter which rings to warn that the end of the line is approaching. When the bell rings you make a decision whether the next word is too long to fit on the line. In the same way, the Editor uses a hot zone to help you decide whether to hyphenate a word or move it to the next line. If the last word on a line extends beyond the hot zone, it becomes a candidate for hyphenation. Once you've defined the hot zone, the Editor will point out words in the text that exceed the zone and suggest where to hyphenate. You can either accept the hyphenation suggestion, place a hyphen elsewhere or not hyphenate at all.

A practical piece of advice: it's a waste of time to hyphenate before you complete all your editing. Even a minor editorial change can change the length of subsequent lines requiring you to readjust all the hyphens in the remainder of the paragraph. If you change print size or reformat the margins, the hyphenation for the entire document will need to be redone. And you've got better things to do. Moreover, some word processing programs do not automatically remove the hyphens from the parts of the text you've changed. So you have to remove the old hyphens before rehyphenating. Remember the global search and replace command I talked about in Chapter 3? You guessed it. It's another way to remove unwanted hyphens (sounds like an ad for removing unwanted facial hair).

Programs with better hyphenation routines do not require hyphenation removal. They will take hyphenation information you enter and create what are called soft or *ghost hyphens*. Ghost hyphen. mark where words can be hyphenated legitimately, but actually hyphenate only if those words exceed the hot zone. I handle hyphenation on my system with a hyphenation program that contains a dictionary and set of hyphenation rules. I have this program place ghost hyphens in all words longer than six characters, and then I ignore the hyphenation problem because all possible words are correctly marked. The program is very accurate and creates the proper hyphenation points for the Editor to use. Some word processors include these kind of hyphenation programs, but they are very expensive.

Boilerplate and List Processing

Boilerplate is a welding term derived from the days when boilers were constructed by riveting together standard sheets of metal. As an editing term, it refers to a document constructed of standard passages or paragraphs. It also refers to a standard piece of text that will be used over and over again, with perhaps minor changes. For example, boilerplate sections can be used in a form letter addressed to many different people or in a standard contract needing some minor changes to fit another application.

Boilerplate is used in all those "personal" letters which inform you that you are the lucky winner of a free weekend in Kuala Lumpur (not including airfare) and which use your name in the text over and over again. The boilerplate part is the standard letter. They (whoever "they" are) make it look personalized by typing in special code names where personal information will be placed. Then the personal information is inserted either manually using the search and replace techniques described in Chapter 3, or automatically during printout by a special program which replaces the code names in the text with actual names and addresses from a storage file list. This technique is called *list processing*.

An additional text file called a *control file* is required to specify whether the whole list or portions are to be used. Organizations doing extensive list processing work use very sophisticated auxiliary programs for creating and maintaining their lists.

Insurance companies and legal firms use boilerplate to construct policies and contracts, combining standard clauses and individual information stored in text files. The typing and changing of contracts then becomes a simple choice of which "plates" to rivet together.

Forms Routines

Many repetitive tasks, such as monthly inventory reports and sales invoices, require entry of information onto standard printed forms. To do this some word processors have a way to indicate where the various information is to be entered. Setting up the format for a form is called "echoing the procedure." You do this by entering information giving the print positions, or by going through the form once with the machine—using the keyboard in conjunction with the printer to indicate where the typed characters are to be placed. The system will then set up a standard screen to prompt you for the required entry information, item for item. As you type each item the cursor moves to the next. Made a mistake?

Move the cursor and correct it. No need to ever jockey a typewriter carriage to the correct position. You just enter the items one after another and, when you're finished, the page is printed with everything where it belongs.

Arithmetic Functions

An arithmetic function incorporated into the word processing package enables you to add, subtract, multiply, and divide within the body of a document. For example, you can define a number at the bottom of a column of numbers to always contain the sum of the numbers in the table. If you change any number in the table, the resulting sum will automatically change. This type of function is very useful in reports containing accounting information or in preparing invoices.

Proportional Printing

I am including this as an advanced feature because it is probably the most frequently misunderstood word processing concept. Proportional printing involves printing each character in a space proportional to its size. The character "M" may be twice the size of an "i". Most typewriters print all characters in equal size spaces. Remember the pica definitions? 10 pica was 10 characters printed in each inch, whether you're printing i's or M's.

To print proportionally, both your word processor and printer must be capable of what is called *incremental movement*. This means the Editor must be able to move the print mechanism in increments of, say, 1/120'' to set up the variable space required for each character. Without a variable spacing or precision printer it will be impossible to do proportional printing.

Most popular word processors are set up to work with a fixed number of characters on each printed line and are referred to as *line oriented* systems. Proportional printing between fixed margins uses a different number of characters on each line. For this reason, word processors that do proportional printing are referred to as *character oriented.* If a line oriented system is used with a proportional printer a very erratic print format results.

A line oriented system cannot create proportionally printed text with flush left and right margins. The character oriented systems use a *space table* containing character widths for all the printable characters. The Editor uses this table to determine how many characters it will take to fill up a line. If you change printers you have to change the values in the table. In addition, the margins are entered in inches or centimeters rather than characters, since the number of characters no longer has a relationship to the margin width. The better character oriented systems will let you see the text the way it will look when printed so that you can make hyphenation and page ending decisions.

One of the more popular word processors circumvents the whole issue by claiming to do what they call *microjustified* printing. This system is line oriented and places letters like the letter "i" in a slightly smaller space than other letters.

You can determine if a word processor is character oriented by the way it sets margins. If the setting is determined by the number of characters on a line it is line oriented, and any attempt at proportional printing will be clumsy at best. The systems claiming to support proportional printing with margins in inches are the ones to get, if true proportional printing is what you want.

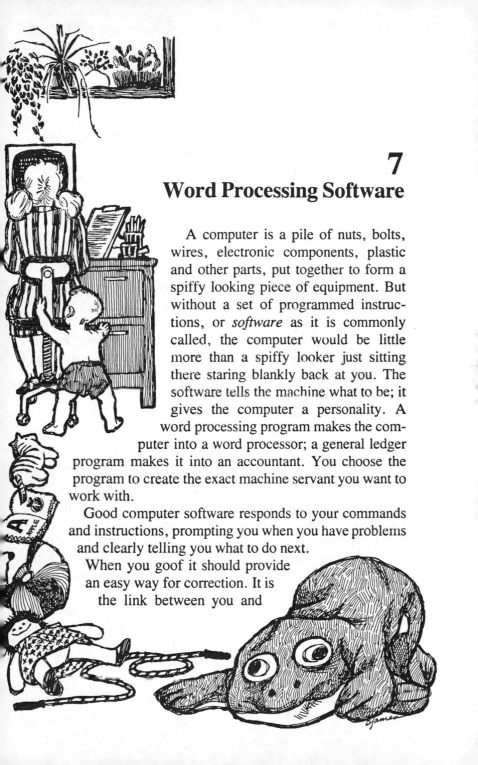

7
Word Processing Software

A computer is a pile of nuts, bolts, wires, electronic components, plastic and other parts, put together to form a spiffy looking piece of equipment. But without a set of programmed instructions, or *software* as it is commonly called, the computer would be little more than a spiffy looker just sitting there staring blankly back at you. The software tells the machine what to be; it gives the computer a personality. A word processing program makes the computer into a word processor; a general ledger program makes it into an accountant. You choose the program to create the exact machine servant you want to work with.

Good computer software responds to your commands and instructions, prompting you when you have problems and clearly telling you what to do next. When you goof it should provide an easy way for correction. It is the link between you and the electronic writing machine: it is the soul of the system, the part that you ultimately come to love or hate.

Put the Software Before the Cart

Time now for the cardinal rule of computers: first choose the best of the available software for your needs, then buy a machine to run it on. Remember, the software is the reason you decide to buy a machine in the first place. Do it the other way and you've put the cart before the horse (and it's pretty hard for a horse to push a cart). Beware! Many computer and word processor salespeople will try to sell you a spiffy looker first. I guess it's a lot easier to talk about the feel of the keys than it is to talk about the intangibles like computer software. Stick to your guns and get your software questions answered first. While hardware is important, your starting point must always be finding the right word processing program with which to bring it alive. You want the right program for your style and your writing needs.

More About Computer Software

There are two types of programs available for use on all computers: *systems* and *applications* programs. If you envision the workings of a computer as a theater or an arena, the primary systems program, called the *operating system*, would be the support personnel, the carpenters, electricians, stage hands, lighting and sound crew, and all the other activities that let the production take place. And the applications program is the production, the actual presentation. When you turn the machine on, the operating system is loaded into the beginning of the program memory area. This is like the stage crew arriving on location, cleaning up, checking out systems and getting ready for the arrival of the stage set and actors. You press the LOAD or START key and the application program is brought into the computer's program storage area from the systems disk. The house lights come up and, if the applications program is a word processor, the Editor and its cohorts come to life.

Why all this talk about systems programs and operating systems in a book on word processing? Because every computer system uses an operating system to carry out basic functions, such as reading from and writing information on the floppy disks, displaying text on the screen or printing it on the printer. Most important, however, is that the type of operating system that comes with a machine establishes the available programs you can run on it.

The most common operating system for small computers and word processing systems (used by only one person at a time) is called CP/M (Control Program for Microcomputers). Getting a CP/M compatible operating system is a smart move because it allows you to choose from a large number of not only word processing but other programs to use with your machine. The standard operating system for medium-size systems (for those of you working with large text files) are CP/M-86 and MS-DOS. The standard operating system for the large systems (ones that work with more than one person at a time) are either UNIX or MPM/86. These mulitiple user operating systems are like a large theater building with many stages: they can run and present several productions at the same time.

Whew! With all that said, let's take a look at the class of application programs that do word processing—the reason you buy a computer.

Word Processor Software

Word processor programs come in three price ranges with capabilities varing accordingly. Low-cost programs cost under $150, mid-range $150 to $500, and high-cost packages from $500 to many thousands of dollars. At this point all you have to do is browse through the glowing descriptions of each category and see which would best serve your type of word processing without making you pay for a lot of unnecessary fringe items.

Low-Cost Programs
These programs are designed to handle documents that are 10 to 12 pages long (double spaced). They are good for beginners be-

cause there are a limited number of functions to learn. They contain all the standard text entry features such as word wrap, cursor control, text scrolling, and the basic editing functions including delete, insert, cut and paste, and search and replace. They'll also do headers, footers and automatic page numbering. File handling capabilities include adding a second document to one being edited, and letting you continue editing after saving a file. These basic editing packages are not fancy or especially flexible, but they will get the small job done.

But the low-cost programs have several major shortcomings because the amount of text they can handle is limited to the size of the machine's text storage memory. Therefore, anything you type that exceeds 10 to 15 pages must be segmented into separate files. You can piece these segments together later when you print, but this is often inconvenient because the text that is displayed on the screen may not have the same margins and page breaks as the printed copy. This means that you won't know where the actual page breaks are until you get a printout. Inconvenient, yes, because you have to print out all the segmented files to find the page endings and then re-combine the files so that each file ends at the end of a page before you reprint. With a low-cost system you are also limited in printing options available. They offer nothing fancy, just straight printing.

If you're operating on a low budget and need a word processor for correspondence or for draft copy of larger documents, a low-cost program may be the way for you to get started. I used one to write the first draft of this book and it worked well. This software package is generally used with machines costing under $1,000. These machines usually have one disk drive or use an audio cassette for text storage. The cost saving of the cassette cannot make up for the inconvenience. Try it for yourself and you'll see what I mean.

The Mid-Range Programs

The editing features of mid-range systems are flexible and easy to use. You can move the cursor by character, word, sentence or paragraph. The delete and insert options let you change your mind about commands just entered. The search and replace mode will let you define in great detail what you want the system to search for: upper- or lower-case letters, complete or partial words—and some will even let you search backwards. Function keys can be set to issue frequently used control commands with a single keystroke— a great time saver!

Mid-range programs let you work with a large number of pages before you have to segment them into separate files. As a matter of fact, they limit document size to the number of pages that can be stored on a file storage disk rather than just the available computer memory. I figure that the maximum-size document should be as large as 30 to 40 percent of the total disk storage area, leaving space on the disk for a duplicate version and some work space. The maximum document size is related to the physical disk you're using. For floppys this could be from 20 to 200 pages of text.

Mid-range programs come with automatic file backup so that when you start to edit a document a duplicate of your original is made. All editing changes are then made on this copy. If a power or system failure screws up a file while you're editing you have the original version to return to. The security of the backup feature more than makes up for the loss of available disk storage space. I wouldn't have it any other way.

These systems are usually operated from a menu, making it easy for beginners. but the same menus and prompting systems so vital to the novice can drive an experienced user crazy. Well-designed systems avoid this by allowing you to specify the amount of help and prompting you need.

There are a lot of options for formatting what you've typed. You get to choose pitch (the number of characters per inch) and line spacing as well as the ability to change the print size for headings and titles. You can also control the printer to do super and subscripts, boldface and overprinting, as well as text justification— left, right, center and space justified.

Some of these systems allow you to view the text on the screen as it will appear when printed, others don't. Systems that offer this option use more memory space for program storage, thereby reducing the text storage area, while the systems that do not show the text as it will be printed are faster and more flexible. It's a trade-off, but I prefer a word processor that shows me what I'll be getting on paper. But remember, even if the software shows you how the text will look when printed, it won't show you things like space justification, subscripts or character size on the screen because all but the most expensive video displays show the characters in *fixed* positions. In other words, the video display screen is like a typewriter with a fixed number of characters on each line.

The file options include the ability to delete files and to read and write text to other files while you edit. This feature is vital if you are revising text by moving portions from one chapter or file to another. The delete file command is vital for those times when you attempt to save a file to a disk that has just run out of space. Deleting a backup or an unnecessary file may free up enough space to let you complete the job.

High-Cost Programs

These are the Mercedes of the word processing programs. They come with, or are sold for, the stand-alone word processor or large-scale mini-computer systems, and are designed for high-volume production or large-size document creation and storage. The editing features are extremely flexible and easy to use with screen display of a full-size page.

Another special feature is dual-page display, allowing you to view and scroll through two pages at a time. These systems have automatic hyphenation entry and removal, as well as flexible paragraph formatting and reformatting. And some even include proportional printing.

Up to 100,000 word automatic dictionary programs are included to help you correct spelling and typing errors. Some systems include indexing programs to automatically create indexes, arithmetic functions to compute the sums and products of numbers entered into tables and, of course, boilerplate routines so you can construct documents from standard paragraphs. Also there are *mail merge* options for generating mailing lists or creating form letters from files containing name and address information.

The file handling is generally geared to large-scale hard disk storage devices which can store many millions of characters. Floppy disk drives, on the other hand, can store merely several hundred thousand. Document names can be an amazing 80 characters long with additional space provided for a description of what's in the file. They keep track of the date when a file was created and the date it was last used, as well as the actual file size (the amount of text stored in the file). In addition, the document handling procedures include automatic search functions to find every document stored on a disk that contains a given word or phrase. This means that I can look at every document that contains the word *rutabaga*. If you want options, a high-cost program will give them to you.

This luxury software attains full potential when it's part of a major information network or if it has the power to communicate with other word processors or computers. For more details, see Chapter 15.

Utility Packages

Independent of size, computer operating systems usually come with *utility programs*—programs that work with the operating system to help you manage your disk files. They are like file clerks. The utility programs are especially important if you are using a low-cost software package which usually has no provision for even a simple function like deleting a text file. So look carefully at the utility programs that are available for the system you are considering. What can they do and what other types of functions can be purchased? At minimum, the operating system utility program should be able to do the following:

1) Format new disks.

2) Erase or delete files.

3) Duplicate entire disks to create backup files.

4) List disk file names and size on the video screen or on the printer.

5) Copy files from one disk to another with verification.

6) Create files with your code word for security.

7) Automatically lock out segments of the disk that have physical problems.

8) Rename a file and change code words.

The operating systems and utility programs generally contain additional functions for data processing applications, many of which are not directly used for word processing. One of these, a *sort utility*, is invaluable for organizing mailing lists when used with the file merging capability of the luxury model word processing systems. And there are other features too.

What Other Software Packages Can You Use?

Besides word processing, your computer or word processor can run a whole series of other types of applications programs. You can buy programs that enable your machine to assume many different personalities. There are low-cost, well-written, easy-to-learn business programs such as accounts receivable, general ledger, and payroll. Everybody who sells or makes computer hardware will gladly tell you about all the software packages available to run on their machines. Again, when you look these over, make sure they are as easy to use as your stereo system.

Remember, you are the only one who knows what needs to be done. Write a job description for a program that will fill your bill. *You're* the expert on your needs! And before buying any word processor find out what other programs are available to run on the system that you invest in. Use the next chapter as a guide, and make sure that later on you will be able to use your machine for more than just word processing. And remember what the great Computer Guru once said: "The bitter taste of poor quality lingers after the sweet taste of low price has faded."

8
Software
For More Than
Just Word Processing

In this chapter we'll look at some inexpensive, easy-to-learn computer programs that can give your computer other useful personalities. Recently, computer users have been dividing themselves into two camps: those who use computers for word processing (working with words and text) and those who use computers for data processing (working with numbers). A third group, those who use their machines to work with both numbers and words, are doing *information processing.* If you look at recent trade journal advertisements you'll find companies who previously advertised only word processing equipment now claiming their machines can be used for both word and data processing. At the same time, computer manufacturers now push the word processing software available for their machines. Obviously, each side is trying to capture a portion of the other's market. You and I know that it doesn't matter what you call the machine; it is the software that brings it to life. The fact is, a lot of companies offer identical programs that have been customized for their machines. What *we* are really concerned with is how easy these programs are to use and whether they'll meet your needs.

Some Software Facts

Because this chapter is concerned with evaluating, selecting and purchasing computer software, let's start with some basic but too frequently misunderstood facts about software.

You'll be surprised to know that when you finally decide on a computer program and purchase it, you are not, in fact, purchasing the program. What you are buying is a license to use the program on a single machine. What if your company has more than one machine? According to law you must purchase a separate copy for each machine. However, an awful lot of people disregard copyright laws the same way they disregard income tax rules. If I had a dollar for every program that is used on machines other than the one for which it was licensed, I could retire today. One large software company estimates that four copies of their programs are being used for each copy sold. The other three copies are run on other machines, or sold or loaned to friends.

Most licenses allow you to make duplicate copies of the program for backup and archiving purposes. In fact, the first thing you should do when you receive a program is to make at least one copy of it. Never work with the original program disk. Now here is an interesting legal fact regarding backup copies of programs: you own the *disk* the program is stored on, but the software company

Here's a typical software license agreement as drawn up by Digital Research of Pacific Grove, California

---

SOFTWARE LICENSE AGREEMENT

IMPORTANT: All of our company's programs are sold only on the condition that the purchaser agrees to the following license. READ THIS LICENSE CARE-FULLY. If you do not agree to the terms contained in this license, return the packaged diskette UNOPENED to your distributor and your purchase price will be refunded. If you agree to the terms contained in this license, fill out the REGISTRA-TION information and RETURN by mail.

_____ (Company) agrees to grant and the Customer agrees to accept on the following terms and conditions nontransferable and nonexclusive licenses to use the software program(s) (Licensed Programs) herein delivered with this agreement.

TERM:

This agreement is effective from the date of receipt of the above-referenced program(s) and shall remain in force until terminated by the customer upon one month's prior written notice or by _____ as provided below.

Any license under this Agreement may be discontinued by the Customer at any time upon on month's prior written notice. _____ may discontinue any license or terminate this Agreement if the Customer fails to comply with any of the terms and conditions of this Agreement.

LICENSE:

Each program license granted under this Agreement authorizes the Customer to use the Licensed Program in any machine readable form on any single computer system (referred to as System). A separate license is required for each System on which the Licensed Program will be used.

This Agreement and any of the licenses, programs or materials to which it applies may not be assigned, sublicensed or otherwise transferred by the Customer without prior written consent from _____. No right to print or copy, in whole or in part, the Licensed Programs is granted except as hereinafter expressly provided.

PERMISSION TO COPY OR MODIFY LICENSED PROGRAMS:

The customer shall not copy, in whole or in part, any Licensed Programs which are provided by _____ in printed form under this Agreement. Additional copies of printed materials may be acquired from _____.

Any Licensed Programs which are provided by _____ in machine readable form may be copied in whole or in part, in printed or machine readable form in sufficient number for use by the Customer with the designated System, to under-stand the contents of such machine readable material, to modify the Licensed Program as provided below, for back-up purposes, or for archive purposes, pro-vided, however, that no more than five (5) printed copies will be in existence under any license at any one time without prior written consent from _____. The Customer agrees to maintain appropriate records of the number and location of all such copies of Licensed Programs. The original, and any copies of the Licensed Programs, in whole or in part, which are made by the Customer shall be the property

(over)

of _____. This does not imply, of course, that _____ owns the media on which the Licensed Programs are recorded. The Customer may modify any machine readable form of the Licensed Programs for his own use and merge it into other program material to form an updated work, provided that, upon discontinuance of the license for such Licensed Program, the Licensed Program supplied by _____ will be completely removed from the updated work. Any portion of the Licensed Program included in an updated work shall be used only on the designated System and shall remain subject to all other terms of this Agreement.

The Customer agrees to reproduce and include the copyright notice of _____ on all copies, in whole or in part, in any form, including partial copies of modifications, of Licensed Programs made hereunder.

PROTECTION AND SECURITY:

The customer agrees not to provide or otherwise make available any Licensed Program including but not limited to program listings, object code and source code, in any form, to any person other than Customer or _____ employees, without prior written consent from _____, except with the Customer's permission for purposes specifically related to the Customer's use of the Licensed Program.

DISCONTINUANCE:

Within one month after the date of discontinuance of any license under this Agreement, the Customer will furnish _____ a certificate certifying that through his best effort, and to the best of his knowledge, the original and all copies, in whole or in part, in any form, including partial copies in modifications, of the Licensed Program received from _____ or made in connection with such license have been destroyed, except that, upon prior written authorization from _____, the Customer may retain a copy for archive purposes.

DISCLAIMER OF WARRANTY:

_____ makes no warranties with respect to the Licensed Programs. The sole obligation of _____ shall be to make available all published modifications or updates made by _____ to Licensed Programs which are published within one (1) year from date of purchase, provided Customer has returned the Registration Card delivered with the Licensed Program.

LIMITATION OF LIABILITY:

THE FOREGOING WARRANTY IS IN LIEU OF ALL OTHER WARRAN-TIES, EXPRESSED OR IMPLIED, INCLUDING, BUT NOT LIMITED TO, THE IMPLIED WARRANTIES OF MERCHANTABILITY AND FITNESS FOR A PARTICULAR PURPOSE. IN NO EVENT WILL _____ BE LIABLE FOR CONSEQUENTIAL DAMAGES EVEN IF _____ HAS BEEN ADVISED OF THE POSSIBILITY OF SUCH DAMAGES.

owns the electronic *information* stored on your disk. You are legally responsible for all backup copies of licensed programs. So be aware of the licensing agreement details for any software package you're considering. A rare few will allow you to use them on multiple machines.

There is a whole series of programs deemed to be "in the public domain," meaning they are free. The only restriction on their use is they may not be sold. Public domain software packages are usually found through local dealerships, user groups or electronic bulletin boards. Check Appendix III for leads on finding a local source. For the most part, user groups offer you some extremely valuable utility and communications programs, as well as a slew of game programs. A lot of the utility programs I use daily were obtained free from the local users group for my machine. These include file copy and backup programs, text compression programs, an indexing program and my beloved communications program. Public domain programs are definitely worth the price you don't pay for them.

General Purpose Software Basics

Here are some things to do and some questions to answer before purchasing a computer program:

1. Be sure you understand the function of the program—what it will actually do, rather than what you hope it will do. Check magazines such as *InfoWorld* for reviews of any software you might be considering.

2. Look very carefully at the manuals and documentation provided with the program. Can you understand them?

3. Get a demonstration of the program. Is it simple to work with? Are there prompting menus? Can you use it after only a brief period of instruction? Find at least one person who is actually using the program on a machine similar to yours. Call and get the inside scoop.

4. Are there low-cost classes available for the program you're considering? A good class could save you hours of frustrating time searching through manuals, and it will get you quickly acquainted

with a lot of the fine points of the system. Costs vary, but computer stores are starting to offer classes for $50-$100. Be sure to check the credentials of the instructor and the course. Talk to some people who have been through it already. I've met many really good instructors as well as a lot of instructors with minimal background in the workings of computer programs and no idea of how to teach effectively. As we all recall from our school days, a poor instructor can set you up for a lifetime of distaste for their subject. If possible, talk to the instructor before you sign up for the class.

5. How long has the software company been in business? How many copies of the program have been sold? What's the reputation of the company and the program? Newly released programs often have lots of problems with them. Sometimes the problems are so severe that the company goes out of business. So don't purchase a program that has been on the market for less than a year. Look beyond company brochures. Is there a toll-free number (800 number) to call if you have problems?

6. What are the costs of updates? Will you be notified when the company updates a program you purchased? Due to the competitive nature of the market, most popular programs are updated every 18 months on the average.

7. Is there a trial period on the software? Many organizations are offering a 30-day trial period with their programs. This is the ideal way to buy a program. There is nothing like being able to try it before you buy it. The only thing you might waste is time, not money *and* time, as the case would be if you purchased the program outright.

8. If you know what program you want the mail order discount software houses could save you some money. Check through the more popular computer magazines for prices. Then do some bargaining with your local dealer. See if he or she will match the price or, better yet, throw in some free classes if you purchase the program from them.

Some Popular Software Packages

This section does not have as many operating descriptions or selection criteria as the word processing sections. But it will help you understand what many of the advertised computer programs are really about and how they can be made to work with your word processor. Let's start with the *calculation spreadsheets*.

Calculation Spreadsheet

Spreadsheets were the first easy-to-use systems for performing mathematical operations (mainly addition, subtraction and multiplication) on tables of numbers. If a word processor is like an editor who helps to create, edit, store, and print text, then a calculation spreadsheet is like an accountant or calculator that'll help to create, store, edit, print and carry out arithmetic operations on numbers.

Let's look at Calc's (the spreadsheet's) personality. Like all good accountants, her domain is a grid or table of rectangular boxes or cells. Boxes running across the page are identified by row numbers and boxes running down the page are identified by column numbers. Let's say that each column is labeled for reference by the letters A through Z and each of the rows are labeled numerically 1 thru 50. This gives 1300 (26 times 50) boxes in which to put labels or numbers. Now a video display screen can't display the complete table at one time. So, in the same way that the Editor lets you scroll through text, Calc can scroll her worksheet both horizontally and vertically behind the video looking glass.

The spreadsheet program doesn't move the cursor from character to character as the word processor does; it moves it from box to box. Up arrow moves it up, side arrow moves it from side to side. You can think of the system as a large map with horizontal and vertical grids to let you know what block you're on. So, instead of living on 12th Street and Avenue A the way some people in New York do, a number in the spreadsheet will reside at box 12A (or is it "12th and A?") The cursor points to the box that it is ready to work with. Want to move to another address? Just press one of the arrow keys.

Calc will let you put one of three things into any of the boxes: titles or non-numeric descriptions (used for indicating what is in a row or column), numbers (with or without decimal points), and *operators*. Operators allow you to enter formulas that will calculate new numbers from numbers in other boxes in the table. The simplest way to show you how it works is to show you how it works . . .

An Example: Let's use the spreadsheet program to analyze expenditures for a word processor. Follow along with Figure 1. First, we'll enter descriptive names for each of the rows in the first column, column A. The first box will be named "Cash Available." The rows below this box contain the various items that have

Figure 1

	A	B
1	Cash Available	
2	Computer	
3	Printer	
4	Software	
5	Disks	
6	Misc. Supplies	
7	Total Costs	1.05*SUM(B2:B6)
8	Balance	SUM(B1-B7)

to be purchased. After typing each entry press the return key and the cursor will move to the box below. Next we enter the mathematical operations we want Calc to do. First the numbers placed in boxes B2, B3, B4, B5 and B6 must be added together and the result placed in box B7. So, move the cursor to box B7 and type the words SUM(B2:B6). You've just told Calc to calculate the sum of the numbers in boxes B2 through B6. But, this really isn't the total amount you'll actually need because we forgot to add in sales tax. Around here that's 5%. The total cost will be 5% greater than the sum of the cost of the items. (This last sentence sounds like something I once learned in high school geometry class.) Move the cursor to the beginning of box B7 and type: 1.05*SUM(B2:B6). In box B8 we want to see the money left over or the amount overspent—the balance. This is the difference between the amount we started with in B1 (cash available) and the total amount to be spent (total cost) in B7. So, in B8 enter the formula SUM(B1-B7) to subtract B7 from B1. That's it! Now we're ready to put some numbers in.

Just be aware that Calc places zeros in every box that does not contain a formula or operator. Move the cursor to B1, which represents the amount of cash available to purchase a system. Let's say you have $2400 available; so type 2400, and press the return key. Presto! 2400 appears in boxes B1 and B8. "Why in B8?" you ask. Box B8 will always show the amount of money available minus what's been spent. At this point the expenditure boxes all have zeros in them, so 2400 − 0 is 2400 and that's the number that's there.

Let's say we have found a low-cost (actually rock bottom) new machine with software, two disk drives and a VDT for $1500. Enter that number in box B2. Presto changeo! Now B2 has 1500 in it, Box B7 shows 1575 (remember the tax), and B8 shows the amount remaining, or 825. The numbers in the sum boxes demonstrate the fact that at any given time the calculation boxes will reflect the numbers stored in the table. You can ask Calc all kinds of "what if" questions, such as what if a box of paper costs $30, and a box of disks cost $20? As soon as you finish entering the numbers, the spreadsheet program makes the calculations and gives you the answers. When you're finished calculating, entering a single command prints the table or stores it as a disk file for later use.

This example is a simple one in that it uses only 8 rows and 2 columns. The real power and utility of the spreadsheets comes when you use, say, 50 rows by 30 columns for entering itemized expenses on an accounting sheet for business profit and loss projections.

Figure 2 shows the minimum you could expect to pay for a word processor. What do you do with the $352.50 remaining? Get the cable that was not included in the price of the printer and the best chair and work table you can find, or get a good light and some shades.

Figure 2

	A	B
1	CASH	2400
2	Computer	1500
3	Printer	400
4	Software	0
5	Disks	20
6	Misc. Supplies	30
7	TOTAL	2047.50
8	Remaining	352.50

Choosing a Spreadsheet Program. The success of Visicalc, the first calculation spreadsheet, was so dramatic that it and the Apple Computer have become household words. When IBM introduced its first personal computer they used a Charlie Chaplin look-alike to marvel over what their machine could do. Well, as we now know, there was nothing marvelous about their machine. He was only plugging yet another machine that used the Visicalc program. The success of Visicalc led other companies to create a whole series of Visicalc look-alikes or, as I like to call them, *visiclones*. The visiclones such as Supercalc, Calcstar and Multiplan made the spreadsheet easier to use and more flexible. In fact, they have made things so much more flexible that Visicalc was updated to Super Visicalc to withstand the competition. Presently in the Calc Wars battle everybody is creating super super clones. So is one clone as good as another? As you read the manufacturers' hype about their comparative advantages, you'll probably find yourself bewildered. I've discovered there's not a lot of difference between these spreadsheet versions—so stick with a name brand in its second generation.

There are four basic questions to ask about a spreadsheet:

1) Are there enough available boxes to do what you want to do?
2) Is it easy to learn?

3) How good are the instruction manuals?

4) Can your word processing program read and work with the stored worksheet tables?

As always, choosing the right package for your purposes involves compromise, so don't get hooked on the special features. A super-super package usually has so many options that it becomes cumbersome to use. If your applications do not require using all the extras, you'll be unnecessarily paying for them in money and in learning time. Lots of people are using the plain vanilla packages and loving them.

I'll say it once again. Whatever Calc program you choose, make sure the disk storage file spreadsheets created by the program can be read by your word processing program. If the computation tables you generate will ever be part of a report, these files must be readable by the Editor.

Data Base Managers (DBM)

This is a fancy name given to a class of programs that enable you to create, store, organize and print files of information. Here are some definitions: a *data base file* consists of a set of common information broken up into what are called records. A *record* is a group of individual fields or items. For example, I have two address files on my machine, one listing friends and another business acquaintances. Both files have one record for each person. Each record consists of a name field, an address field and a telephone number field. Think of the file as a large file box containing a series of compartments, each of which is divided into a group of smaller sections holding stored information. Or think of it as an apartment building with different records occupying each of the apartments.

In the same way the word processor responds like an *editor* and the spreadsheet like a *calculator,* the data base manager is like a file clerk or file *manager.* The Manager's job is to help you define and start or create new files; add to, display and edit existing files; and print or store summaries of stored information. To create a file you must define the component parts of the records that will make up the file. This means naming and setting up space in the apartment building. Once you define the form of the compartments, all the levels or records will have that same form. Let's take a look at how it all might work.

Once you've loaded in the data base program from the systems drive the Manager takes over, sets up the act and then asks what you'd like to do. To enter a new file, you enter the command CREATE. The Manager then calls up the Creator and it displays instructions that ask you to enter the file name and the filed definitions. Let's create a name and address file and call it AD-BOOK. Type in the name ADBOOK.

The Creator then requests a name for each of the fields that will be within the record and the maximum number of characters that'll be put in each field. An address file looks like an address book so, let's call the first field NAME. This will be the line on which the names are typed. So how do you figure out the maximum number of characters for the name field? Hmm . . . Who do we know with the longest name? Ah yes, Questionable Qwenton Qwerty III has 31 letters in his name. So the field called NAME should be at least 31 characters wide if Qwerty is to be listed in full regalia. By going through a similar process we add a 20-character address field called ADDRESS, a 22-character field called CITYSTATEZIP containing the rest of the address, and a 10-character field for phone numbers including area codes (no space or dash). Now we've defined all the fields necessary for this file.

Pressing the return key indicates that the definitions are correct and complete, and then in a wink (or a nod) the Creator creates a structure for the data base. In other words, the Creator creates a structure for the apartment building. Then the Manager checks to see if information is to be placed into the compartments. If you wish to enter some names, addresses, and phone numbers you can do so with helpful prompts supplied by the DATA ENTRY module. Just keep entering names, addresses and phone numbers until you've gone through your entire address book. As you enter them they are placed into their proper compartments.

The real fun of working with a data base manager comes after the information is entered. Using the scrolling keys you can move through the data structure field by field, inserting, deleting and editing the information. With a SORT command you can sort the file according to last name, phone number, area code or zip code. You can store the complete file or a portion of it on a floppy disk. You can instruct the Manager to print out the whole file or important segments, such as everyone whose last name is Smith or Qwerty. Most good DBM packages will allow several searches to be carried out sequentially so you can select records under multiple conditions, such as every one of your customers with the name Jones in zip code 50510. The DBM programming languages which come with the program are easy to learn because they use simple and powerful descriptive commands. I wouldn't consider programming in any other type of language.

Now that you've got the gist, let's go over how you select a data base program.

Data Base Managers Bottom Line

If you will be using both a calculation spreadsheet and a data base manager, be sure the disk storage files from both programs can be read by the other. Both programs store information in boxes or compartments, and many systems offer compatible disk files. Of course the Manager's files and reports must be accessible and usable by your word processing software. For those of you who keep automated mailing lists or use boilerplate techniques, data base managers are a great way to keep and update your files. For these special uses the functions of the DBM are far superior to those of any word processor.

There are a number of questions to ask while you're looking at and checking out data base managers. What is the maximum number of records that can be stored in a file? With most systems you'll find this is a function of the disk storage your computer or word processor has available for the manager. Using a data base manager is the main reason most people purchase hard disk systems. The thing about floppy disks that drives people crazy is the time required to do something to every record in a huge file, such as sort everything based on what appears in a particular field. I have seen large mailing lists run for hours performing simple operations.

The time may or may not be shortened with a more efficient or faster running program; your system might just require a faster disk drive. Before buying anything, check out the time required for routine operations—such as sorting a file. Will the program allow the merging or combining of two data base files?

Get a demo of the report writing feature that comes with all these systems. Is the report writing feature easy to use? Will it handle arithmetic operations as part of its normal processing? Will it handle everything that you might want to do?

Programs for Business

A lot of companies use a data base management system to set up many of their business functions. Others purchase a *computerized business system*. When should a business consider putting all its accounts onto a computer? I say when either the number of employees goes beyond 20 people or the number of accounts becomes so large that a manual process is either too costly or too slow. The greatest cause of business failure is the lack of timely financial information on the company accounts. Using an accountant may mean you're only getting monthly reports. In 30 days you could find yourself out of business.

No matter what you decide about a computerized business system, you're going to need an accountant to advise you on matters such as equipment capitalization, depreciation, and other tax information. Whatever package you purchase, it'll have to provide your accountant with all the information needed. You can learn to use a word processor just stumbling along. But it's different with a business system. You will either have to work with an accountant or learn accounting yourself. So get your accountant, or hire an accountant as a consultant, to help you select a business system to fit your business.

Don't purchase anything without the assistance of a CPA. This is especially true if your business receipts are stored in a shoe box.

Accounting systems are usually divided into five parts: General Ledger, Accounts Receivable, Accounts Payable, Inventory and Payroll. Call them The Big Five:

General Ledger (not the hero of the Battle of the Bulge) is a record of a company's business functions. It keeps track of revenues, assets, expenses and liabilities. The ledger should allow transactions to be entered and recorded according to department, salesperson, project or any other categories unique to your business. Usually the general ledger will take input from the other four accounting subsections in the form of *journal entries*. If the input and updating are automated, make sure the updates are listed out and checked by a non-machine type employee (a person). The most common accounting technique is called the *balance forward method*. In this, the balance is carried forward each month, closing out the detail for the previous month.

The general ledger will also provide financial reports and security for changes in the master file. It is the source of information required to evaluate the company performance.

Accounts Receivable is what it sounds like—the record of all money owed to the company, by whom it is owed or by whom it has been paid. In addition to integrating with the general ledger, this part of the program produces customer invoices, records cash receipts, produces a listing of customer balances, and pinpoints customers who have reached their credit limit. It handles cash receipts, customer account inquiries, and finance charges. It computes commissions if you want, and integrates order entry procedures.

Accounts Payable is a record of all money owed or paid out by your company. A well-designed system will give you a list of categorized expenditures according to outside supplier or purchase order number. It will determine detailed information on cash requirements, as well as cash projections for future operations. It will prepare and print checks as well as print the check register.

The *Payroll* system will calculate employee wages, including deductions for federal and state taxes, social security, union dues and health insurance. It will print out statements and checks, including year-end taxes.

The *Inventory* portion of an accounting system enables you to track parts on order or in the inventory. It will also input data to the general ledger system.

As should be the case with any system approaching the complexity of a computerized business system, make sure that all functions allow a manual override so that you can make additions to files or alter processing. Security may be another critical issue. Who has access to the system and how are unauthorized people kept out? Ask all these questions and get the answers before purchasing any business system.

The starting point in computerizing a business is usually a general ledger program. Obviously this portion, as well as the rest of the system, should function in the same manner that your manual business procedures do. Whether you decide to purchase the complete Big Five in one shot, or purchase one piece at a time, make sure that the component parts of the system you're considering will all work together. See if the software can be expanded to include a *management information system* to help you do business forecasting like predicting sales, determining when to order materials and when to hire additional people.

Other Programs

Another program you might want is a *calendar program* to help you schedule your time and keep appointments. Larger organizations use these programs to help schedule meetings for large groups of people. This becomes a relatively simple task if everyone's personal calendar is stored in the machine. These programs are valuable for organizing and planning activities.

Also available are a pile of *utility programs* to assist with file handling, maintenance and recovery techniques. Check local user group offerings before purchasing one of the commercial programs. In addition, there is a class of *computer graphic programs* that will let you view information in the form of graphs or pie charts. It's been said that "A picture is worth a thousand numbers," and that's often true. Want more? There are stock market and economic analysis programs, home finance programs, and educational programs to teach you anything you might ever care to learn. And, of course, video games. How do you locate them? Start by browsing through the Appendices.

I believe the most vital programs are the ones that facilitate machine-to-machine communications. This is so important that an entire chapter (Chapter 15) has been devoted to this technology.

Programming on Your Own

Some of you will find that you need to do your own programming, either to modify supplied programs or to create the kind of crazy systems that no one but you would use. Let me spend a little time talking about *programming languages* and what you can expect from some of them. Let's start with some history.

In the beginning, everyone wrote programs (programmed) in the language of 1's and 0's, called *binary* or *machine language.* Then someone invented a new language that would let people program using alphabetic code rather than binary numbers. This language was much easier to use and work with. A program, called an *Assembler,* translated the symbolic instruction or code written by a programmer into binary instructions to be run by the computer. It was a huge step toward simplifying the programming task. I don't know anyone who actually programs in machine language anymore. Assemblers make it so much easier.

Assembler language was then used to create higher level languages called *third generation languages.* These languages were closer to English, enabling programmers to solve many different types of programming problems more easily. The process of translating these higher level languages to either machine or intermediate level languages is called *compilation.* Let's take a look at some of these languages:

The first of the third generation languages was FORTRAN (FORmula TRANslation), developed in the late 1950's to assist scientists who were then the predominant users of computers. The language syntax is based in algebra and is superb for solving mathematical problems. FORTRAN, however, was not the easiest language to teach non-programmers. In the mid-60's a simplified FORTRAN-type language was developed at Dartmouth College to simplify the teaching of programming to freshman science students. Called BASIC, this language has become the most popular and widespread programming language used on small computers and word processors. Though its capabilities have been expanded, it is still an algebraic language, and is fine for teaching students how to program, but not adequate for any serious programming. Yet just about every introductory computer book wastes your time and energy teaching you to program in BASIC.

The most widely used language for business programming is COBOL (Common Business Oriented Language), a language very similar to English. As a matter of fact, COBOL is to business what Hebrew is to religion. And if you'll be programming mathematical problems take a look at APL (A Programming Language), a favorite of mathematicians. PASCAL, much more elegant than BASIC in my opinion, will replace it as the most widely used language. If you're into learning a programming language, definitely look at PASCAL. Those of you who want very efficient assembler-type programming should look at the FORTH or C languages.

Even if you do not intend to do any programming yourself, you should know in what language a program you'll be purchasing is written. Just about all word processor, calculation spreadsheet and data base manager programs are written in Assembler, making them much faster and smaller in size than programs written in the higher level languages. Business systems are usually programmed in COBOL or PASCAL.

One final word: for copyright protection, programs you purchase will be supplied in machine language form, rather than the original source code. So if you want to modify a commercial program to work better for your specific needs, you will have to purchase the actual source code in Assembler, COBOL or PASCAL for a substantial extra cost. The purchase of source code programs and their modification would make another whole book.

The Non-Procedural Language

The problem with all of the programming languages described is that they are procedural in nature and require you to be able to program in order to use them. So the next step was the development of fourth-generation, or *non-procedural languages*. Now we are talking about the programs this book is all about, the ones that turned the computer into a useful tool for We, the People. Languages for word processing, calculation spreadsheets, data base management, communications, and who-knows-what will be coming next. These languages are the important ones for you to learn and use—not the dinosaur languages of the past.

The BASIC language has played a leading role in the history of computer technology but it is of little value today. Ignore any comments you hear coming from the computer historians and educators about the need to learn BASIC. Learning BASIC is as relevant to using a computer as learning Latin is to speaking English. *E Pluribus Unum.*

9
Hardware Configurations

Until now I've focused only on features offered by the word processing software. In this section I'm going to describe the hardware, or machines, that can be used for word processing. These machines are called word processors, text processors or personal computers.

But the mere name doesn't tell much about the machines' capabilities. And to further complicate matters, every computer manufacturer can sell you a machine that'll perform *some* kind of word processing. I've said it before and I'll say it again: whatever hardware and software combination you buy should best support your proposed use of the system. So don't pay for functions you don't need, and don't be chintzy on the vital functions. Make sure the software and hardware that you're considering work well together, and don't assume that just because they are sold together they are the best combination. To increase sales many computer companies are giving away word processing programs with their computers. It's just like buying a stereo system that comes with a set of records. It could be the right stereo with the wrong records. The same is true with a computer system. And I know of several individuals who purchased a number of word processing programs before finding the right one for their computer. But, then again, they did not follow the cardinal rule of computing—choose the software first, then the hardware.

Now let's look at hardware configurations, the various ways word processors are packaged. What you'll find is word processors sold as *electronic typewriters, stand-alone word processing systems, personal computers* or *shared systems*. Here are the details of each.

The Electronic Typewriter

This is an electric typewriter that's controlled by a small computer. Sometimes they're called intelligent typewriters. But they're not geniuses. Their intelligence is limited to making corrections and performing low-level editing.

These machines are the next step up from electric typewriters and they'll ultimately replace the electric as the electric replaced the manual typewriter. They come complete with a keyboard and print mechanism and look very much as their name suggests. The print mechanism is usually a typeball or *daisywheel* (see explanation in Chapter 10) with a print speed of 15-30 characters per second (150-300 words per minute). Speaking of printing, they can usually print in various print sizes and usually will handle proportional printing with space justification. In other words, they produce precision quality print. But more about this in Chapter 10.

The electronic typewriter is a super typewriter that can increase typing productivity, but I'm glad I didn't have to edit this book on one. They're not made for complex editing. Their "window" into the text storage area is very small, displaying only one or two lines.

This makes it difficult to move sentences and large blocks of text. And because you can't see how the page will look until it's printed, you lose flexibility in setting up tables and page formatting. They do offer automatic carriage return, text justification, type over correction, and some machines can even store several pages of text.

Some of the electronic typewriters are portable and about the size of an attache case. Most of these machines will store text on either cassette tape, magnetic cards or floppy disks for later editing and printing. You can figure an electronic to cost about twice as much as a good electric typewriter, that is, between $500 and $3000.

If you are considering an electronic typewriter, check out how easy it is to operate. If there's a chance you will eventually want a more versatile system, see if the machine is "upward compatible." That is, can it be converted into a more advanced machine when you are ready for one? Can a display screen and disk storage drives be added later on? At a minimum, can it be used as a slow-speed printer for a larger system?

The Stand-Alone Word Processor

These are small computers equipped with special keyboards and video displays, designed to be used primarily for word processing. They look very much like the machines described in Chapter 2. They are sold as a complete package of software and hardware. The whole shebang includes keyboard, memory, screen, disk drives, word processing program, operating system, and printer.

Most salespeople I've talked with didn't differentiate between the hardware and the software. They usually described the stand-alone as a single unit, ignoring the fact that the hardware and software are separate entitites. But some vendors do recognize the distinction and sell machines supplied with a "General Purpose Operating System." If you think you'll want to do more than word processing on your machine, ask the salesperson for a list of other programs that run with the machine's operating system. The CP/M or MS-DOS operating systems can be purchased as an option on some of these systems to give you access to a large selection of other software. Find out who else supplies software for the machine you want to buy. Search all the software outfits and computer stores. A good starting point is the software supplier list presented in the resource section Appendix III of this book. The more programs available, the more tasks you and your machine can tackle.

These systems are extremely flexible in their capabilities and very easy to use. They are the choice of organizations that process large quantities of words and have been designed with the secretary in mind. They're the best, as well as the most costly, of the word processing systems.

IBM ads say, "You get what you pay for." But then again, there are people who say that IBM really stands for "I've Been Misled." Look at several of the systems. Note how easy they are to operate and how flexible they are. Make your decision based on what you'll be using the machine for. There is no substitute for smart shopping, which takes time. Stand-alones cost $4,000-$12,000, including a fancy printer.

Personal Computers

A personal computer is a small (in size, but not in capabilities) desk-top machine made for use by one person at a time. Unlike the stand-alone word processor, it doesn't come with a fancy keyboard or printer and you pay separately for any software, including word processing programs. It's like ordering *a la carte*. Once again, first choose the word processing program you want, then buy a small computer that can run it. Find out what other programs are available for your machine's operating system. Believe it or not, the software you buy could easily cost more than the computer itself, especially if you use the machine for something other than word processing. And how could you resist the temptation to do that?

When you go to buy a personal computer, don't pay much attention to the prices you see advertised. These are for bare bones systems, usually just a keyboard and computer to hook up to your TV, not ones configured for word processing. You want the price for a system that includes a video display, at least 48K of memory (see the next chapter), a printer, and, of course, the word processing software. External storage should be *two disk drives*, unless you're on a rock bottom budget and working on short documents; then you might consider one drive or possibly cassette tape for document storage. Add it up: this will be the real price you need for comparison purposes.

You will also find these machines sold as portable systems, fully configured with a small screen and two disk drives, weighing about 24 pounds, and as briefcase models with tape rather than disk storage.

The price of a personal computer system to do word processing will be from $1,000 to $8,000, without a printer. A printer costs anywhere from $300 to $3000.

Multi-Terminal Word Processors

A word processor does your editing so much faster than even Wonder Woman (or is it Wonder Person?) can type, that most of the time the machine is just hanging around waiting for you to press a key. And this is true even when you're typing at full speed. But don't let it bother you—even a 600-word-per-minute printer can't keep the Editor fully occupied! This is why some word processors can print out copy while you're busy editing text on the screen. It's this lightning speed that makes it possible to have two or more typists working simultaneously on one system. Provided, of course, that you've bought two video display terminals and two chairs. This mode of operation is called *shared logic* or *multiuser*. In addition, the total resources of a system—not just the software and memory—can be shared among several users on what is called a *shared resource* or *local area network*. Both shared logic and shared resource systems reduce costs by the sharing of various hardware and software elements among multiple users. Here's some information about these two systems.

Shared Logic Systems

A shared logic system comes in two basic forms. One uses a microcomputer, the same as the stand-alone word processor. The other uses a larger, more powerful machine, the *minicomputer*. The major difference between these systems is the speed at which they operate and the number of typing terminals (or stations) that can be attached. The micro will support two to four typists simultaneously, while the minicomputer can handle as many as 20 typists working at one time. In these systems, the terminals where the typing and editing is done have only limited intelligence, serving as an input station to the computer itself, which could be physically located in another room.

File storage is on a large-scale hard disk, rather than floppys, because of the large volume of material produced by the multiple stations attached to the machine. And though the cost of the hardware is lower per typist, the high cost of a multiuser fancy operating system offsets some of the savings. Besides assisting the Editor, the operating system now has to handle all the complicated swapping around of text for the people using it simultaneously.

For companies thinking of buying a shared logic system, the question to ask is, "How many people can work effectively at the same time on this system?" This is always less than the number of stations that theoretically can be supported by the machine. In the real world, the more typists on the machine at one time, the slower it responds to each typist. Eventually, the machine responds as slowly as the checkout line in a supermarket at 5:30 p.m. on a Friday afternoon.

Shared logic systems cost $5,000 to $100,000; individual work stations cost an extra $500 to $2,000. This is the type of system that would be used by a larger company where word processing terminals could easily be attached to the computer system they've already got. Organizations with high word processing demand might easily justify the purchase of a separate, large-scale shared logic system.

Shared Resource Configuration

If you've ever been in the newsroom of a large newspaper or seen Lou Grant on TV, you've seen a shared resource configuration at work. It differs from the shared logic system in that each of the word processors is a stand-alone word processor, or what is known as an *intelligent terminal*. Each has its own computer and resident word processing program, but they share the most expensive parts of the system—the bulk disk storage and the printer. It is cost-effective if large file storage areas and a high-quality printer are required by more than one work station.

This configuration establishes communal storage files accessed and used by each individual word processor, extending the capabilities of an individual word processor or personal computer. This concept of sharing resources is also known as *networking*. You will find detailed explanations of local area networks and multiprocessing systems in Chapter 16.

10
Hardware Components

Here's where I demystify the computer hardware terms everyone seems to use, but too few really understand. I'll translate the bits and bytes of computer lingo. In addition, the information in this chapter will help you understand the component parts of a packaged system or evaluate component parts that can be purchased separately and fit together to form a word processing system.

The Computer or Processor

Remember my description of the Computer Personality and the Text Storage Area? Well, if you talk to a computer salesperson and use those terms, he or she will think you're crazy. These words are my way of expaining how the machine really works, but it's not the jargon that computer people use. The salesperson may tell you the computer in front of you is ''an 8 bit machine with 64K of RAM, 4K of ROM, and Z-80a processor with a 4 megahertz clock.'' Stay cool! Here's a translation.

The most important part of all this gibberish is the 64K RAM. RAM (pronounced like the animal) stands for *random access memory,* the amount of memory the word processor or computer has in which to store and handle its program, and to use as work area for your text. The K means thousand (actually 1,024), so there are about 64,000 bytes of memory available. Bytes? No, it's not time for lunch. A *byte* is just another name for a character (like A,b,c,1,2,3,#,%,$). So the machine can provide 64,000 characters for the Editor to set up and do its thing with. The 4K of ROM *(read only memory)* is a portion of the computer's memory set aside for use by the machine's operating system. The ROM memory, unlike RAM, is not erased when the power is turned off. It is always there. You can't destroy it; you can only read and use its information. Machines are designed with enough ROM to function and there is no need to be concerned with the details of their operation.

Don't buy a system that has less than 48K bytes of RAM, unless you'll be typing material shorter than 2 or 3 pages long. As a matter of fact, get the largest size memory you can afford. Most systems come with a minimum of 64K bytes. The word processing program you'll choose (before you really start to look hard at the hardware) requires a certain amount of memory to function in. Then it'll need memory as a workspace for the text you'll be typing. Additional memory beyond the sum of these two can be added on at some time in the future. You don't have to buy it all in the beginning.

You don't have to concern yourself with the clock speed or whether the processor is a Z-80a or a 8086. You only want to know if it will operate quickly enough for your needs. The speed you care about is the combined speed of the computer and the software. You want to know how fast the machine loads material to and from the disk, and how long it takes for the system (hardware and software) to do things like search and replace information in a twenty-page document. You're the one who will be working with the machine. Will its response time to do routine tasks satisfy your work habits? All I can suggest is, try the system out with some of your own material before buying it.

Bits and Bytes

Computer systems use a kind of morse code to represent characters, similar to the way a telegraph works. The computer recognizes each character or byte by a code consisting of a combination of eight dots and dashes (or 8 *bits* of information). Most people buying a word processor or computer will get a microcomputer, a machine that works with one character (one byte also known as 8 bits) at a time. In the same way that Grant is buried in Grant's tomb, a microcomputer is also called an 8-bit machine. Now here's what I'm leading up to. Although most word processors are 8-bit machines, there are more powerful 16- or 32-bit machines that are called either *minicomputers* or *super micros*. Minis have large memory storage areas and are faster than micros. If you are setting up a network with a series of word processor stations sharing the same computer, or if you're using gigantic text files you probably would need a super micro. If your company already has a large-scale computer, it's probably a 16- or 32-bit machine and there is a good possibility you can run word processing on it along with its other tasks. The mainframe, an even larger class of machine, works with 32 or more bits (that's 4 bytes) at a time. What a mouthful.

Floppy Disk Drives

The word processing operating procedures in the "how to operate a word processor" chapters were explained using a machine with two floppy disk drives. One drive was used for the system disk and the other for a storage disk to hold the electronic text files. If you are really tight for cash and will be using a fairly simple word processing program, you can get away with only one disk drive. I don't advise it, because with only one drive it's a chore to make backup copies of important disks. If you do get only one drive make sure that a second one can be added later since the more versatile word processing programs usually require two. Most systems will let you use up to four floppy disk drives.

Floppys come in three sizes: an 8-inch standard, a 5½-inch mini, and the recently released 4-inch, or smaller, *microfloppy*. Information is recorded on and read from the disks as magnetized spots on a series of concentric circular tracks on the disk's surface. Don't expect one machine to read information from a floppy written by another brand of machine. There is very little compatibility between the disks from different brands of machines, unless they use compatible operating systems and 8-inch drives. Systems with 5½-inch or smaller drives have no standardization at all. I mention this only to dispel the assumption that most people have that all machines write the same way on disks. They don't!

The microfloppys are a recent addition to the market and range in size from 3 to 4 inches. The disks are housed in a rigid case, making them more durable and reliable than their larger counterparts. The size and capacity of these disks vary from manufacturer to manufacturer. They were intended to evolve into a more durable floppy disk that could fit in a shirt pocket. As I see it, a simpler alternative would have been to get shirt manufacturers to start making 5¼-inch pockets on all shirts. All joking aside, the smaller disk means a smaller drive which, ultimately, will mean smaller and lighter computers for us to have and use.

The storage capacity of a floppy disk is specified in *kilo*bytes; that is, in thousands of characters. Now, be really careful. If you are told a disk can hold 210K bytes of information, make sure this means 210,000 characters of text, not 210,000 total characters. "What's the difference?" you ask. Before a word processor or computer can use a floppy disk, it must write housekeeping, directory, and error detection procedures on it. This *formatting* or initialization process and the setting aside of space for system functions can use 10 to 20 percent of the total available disk storage space. So, a floppy with a total capacity of 210K might only hold

168,000 characters of text. If there are approximately 1500 characters per double-spaced page this translates into about 112 pages rather than 140 pages at 210K.

Before talking to a computer or word processor salesperson, it's a good idea to determine the number of characters in the type of material you write. To do this, count the number of words on a page. My page is based on an average word of five characters plus one stored space after each word. If I double-space, this works out to about 250 words or roughly 1500 characters per page. Make these calculations for your kind of writing. Don't use someone else's estimate, because storage capacity has a way of getting exaggerated.

How much storage do you require? Determine the maximum number of pages you will want to work on at one time. For a writer this would probably be a chapter rather than a whole book. To calculate minimum storage capacity you need, multiply the number of pages times the number of characters per page times three (for backup and workspace). The longest chapter in this book was 20 pages. Twenty pages times 1500 characters per page times three gives a total of 90K as a minimum for the floppy storage. My system has 180K formatted storage on each drive, so I can easily keep two to three chapters with backup on a disk. In addition, the system disk has to be large enough to accommodate the operating system, the word processor program and any other programs you might want to have readily available, such as a dictionary, thesaurus, or hyphenation program. I recommend no less than 180K, and preferably 250K or more.

The first word processing and computer systems used single-density drives which were not especially efficient at storing information. *Double-density drives* are becoming the standard and are worth the slight additional cost because they store twice as much information as their older counterparts. There are also *quad-density drives* that compress the information even further, and drives that can read from both sides of a disk, thereby again doubling the amount of storage. Combining dual-sided readability with a quad-density drive gives you eight times the storage capacity of a single-density drive. Double- and quad-density drives require the use of *high-density disks* which are slightly more expensive than single-density ones.

I'd advise buying a system with double-density drives and weighing the advantage of the quad- and dual-sided system against the additional cost. Here is a table that summarizes the approximate text storage capacity of single-sided floppy disk drives. For double-sided drives, double the table values.

Storage Summary

	Single	Double	Quad	
Standard (8")	250K	500K	1meg	(167-667 pp.)
MiniFloppys (5½")	100K	200K	400K	(67-267 pp.)
Microfloppys (under 4")	—	300K	—	(133 pp.)

Just to give you an idea of what it cost me to write this book: I used 5¼-inch double-density floppy disks. While writing and editing I used three disks plus another three for backup. 5¼-inch disks cost about $2.50 each, so my total cost was $15. Because the disks can be erased and reused, the real cost was even less.

In 1983 single-density minifloppy disk drives cost about $250. Standard floppy drives cost about $400. Dual minifloppy drives (two in one cabinet) start at $500 and dual standard drives start at around $700. Double density adds about 20 percent to the prices. Quads start around $600 or double the single density price. It's incredible that a quad 8-inch disk can hold almost a million characters—a megabyte—of text. That's over 600 pages of material. After writing this book on minifloppies, I would advise all you writers out there to purchase double- or quad-density floppy drives. It just makes for a lot fewer disks to keep track of.

Hard Disks

For those of you who'll need to store large amounts of text without having to change disks, bulk storage *hard disk* units are the thing to use. These devices, used in place of floppys, can store anywhere from five million to 100 million characters of information (formatted of course). This is over 50,000 pages of text. Hard disk prices start at about $1500 and go as high as $20,000, depending on the storage capacity.

Hard disk drives come in two varieties, those with removable and those with fixed storage disks. A hard disk system uses a recording platter made from aluminum rather than flexible plastic. The least costly variety, the *Winchester*, has a fixed platter sealed inside an air-tight drive. In addition to holding a lot more information and being five to ten times faster than floppys, hard disks are a lot more reliable since they are never handled or exposed to contaminants in the air. Unfortunately, they cost around ten times more than floppy disk drives, and *non-removable platter* means that if you run out of storage you can't just slip in another disk; you have to buy another drive. Also, backing up or copying 10 megabytes of information from hard disk onto floppys requires 20 double-density 8-inch disks. That's a lot of floppys and a lot of time. The Winchester manufacturers advise using a second Winchester, a high-speed magnetic tape drive, or a standard home video tape recorder with some special circuitry, to back up all your vital information. So, if you are considering a hard disk system, formulate your backup plans first!

Recently, several manufacturers announced cheapie 5¼-inch and 3.9-inch removable hard disk systems. Yes, I said removable, and with 5-megabyte storage capacity. The unit sells for around $2000. Since the disks are removable, the backup problem may be solved. By the time you get this book these drives will be on the market. They are definitely the bulk storage medium of the future, and when their costs drop low enough, they may even replace floppys.

A hard disk drive costs five to ten times more than a floppy disk drive. But, if you consider the cost per thousand characters of disk storage capacity, both floppy and hard disk drives cost from 20¢ to $2.50 per thousand bytes of storage. On a cost-per-K of storage basis a hard disk drive is a definite bargain.

Printers

By now you all know that the printer prints your text on paper, labels, or your tie if you're not careful. But how does it work? The

Editor sends an electronic representation of your text to the printer in a kind of computer Morse code called ASCII (pronounced Ask-Key). The printer identifies the coded characters and then signals its print mechanism to print them.

Compared to a typist, the printer is extremely fast and reliable. Compared to me, it's Superman. Compared to electronic computer speeds, it is quite slow. The advertised speed of a printer is not what it'll do in your office. These ratings are about as realistic as the EPA gas mileage rating on cars, so use them only for comparison purposes. If you need a real world estimate, figure on about 50-70 percent of the advertised speed. A humble printer will print 50 characters per second or around 500 words per minute.

The printer is the weakest link in the word processing system, and in some cases it'll cost as much as the rest of the word processor put together. It is, by far, the noisiest part. And, to add injury to insult, it's the most likely component to break down because of all its moving parts.

The printer is the one item that you may want to buy separately from the word processor or computer. By buying directly from a manufacturer or discount house you can save some money or obtain a more flexible printer. But, beware—before you purchase a printer make sure it's compatible with the rest of your system and comes with the cables and all the other spaghetti required to attach it. Printers are attached to computers by either a *serial* or a *parallel* connection or interface. Printers using parallel connection are $100 cheaper than printers using serial connection. High quality printers come with both types of connection options. (For more information on serial and parallel connections see Chapter 15.)

If possible, talk to someone who's using the printer in the same way you plan to. Most printer sales people will gladly refer you to someone using one of their machines; you can't beat firsthand information from another person to find out how well something works, and how difficult it was to get it working.

Most printers don't come with a keyboard, but you can have one added for some extra money. If you want a printer with a keyboard, consider an electronic typewriter that interfaces (attaches) to your computer. They're about half the price of a good printer, but about one-third the speed, and not quite as reliable. There's also a kind of Rube Goldberg device that has little plungers that fit over a normal typewriter keyboard and press down on the keys like a mechanical hand in a monster movie. Don't get one of these! Put your money into a more expensive printer rather than the aspirin you'll need for the headache these things will cause.

If you want to turn out camera-ready copy for printing a book or a professional report, you should consider a precision printer capable of proportional spacing. Proportional spacing allows each character as much space as its design requires. It doesn't fit larger and smaller letters into the same standard space like a typewriter does. For example, a capital *B* will get twice the space of a lower-case *i* or *j*. If you want the finished appearance of proportional printing, *be sure* that the word processing software you bought will work with a proportional printer.

Some printers are bi-directional, printing in both forward and reverse directions for increased speed and efficiency. Here again, the word processing software must be able to control direction.

Printers can be purchased with a variety of print styles and sizes. The print size or *pitch* is specified as the number of characters that will be printed per inch. The most common print sizes are 10 characters per inch (Pica), 12 characters per inch (Elite), and 15 characters per inch (Micron). To put this all in real terms, a printer with 10-pitch characters will print 85 characters on each line of an 8½-inch wide page. All the characters will have equal spacing, same as a typewriter.

Letter quality printers come with fixed or incremental spacing. If your work requires proportional printing, make sure the printer is capable of incremental spacing in multiples of 1/120 of an inch and that fonts are available for the printer. This is also required if the printer will be using variable size fonts.

Printers now come with the intelligence to automatically justify text, print proportionally, change character sizes and do graphics. You will find these features worthless unless your word processor can control these functions. There are thousands of people who own printers capable of creating high resolution graphs and pictures but have no way of using this function because their word processors cannot issue the commands.

Impact Printers

The most commonly used printers are *impact printers*. Like a typewriter, they strike or impact a raised character against an inked ribbon to print a character on paper. The two common impact printers are the *printwheel printer* and *dot matrix printer*.

The Printwheel Printer (letter quality printers). The most common of these impact printers is called a *daisy wheel printer*. Not surprisingly, its print element resembles a flattened daisy with raised characters on the tip of each of its 96 petals. When this printer receives a message to print a character, it spins the daisy wheel until that character is in position for printing. A small hammer then shoots out and smacks the petal into the inked ribbon and paper to print the character.

The removable daisy wheels can be purchased in a wide variety of print styles and sizes, including foreign language alphabets. If you'll frequently use more than one print style or size on a page, you should consider buying one of the printers that accommodates more than one daisy wheel at a time. This'll save you the inconvenience of having to be there to change print wheels during printing, a task that could drive even a trained monkey crazy. Daisy wheel printers run at a relatively slow 12-55 characters per second, but their print quality is akin to that of the better electric typewriters. You can expect the cost of a daisy wheel printer to be from $600 to $3,000, depending on speed, the number of characters it can print on each line, and whether it is a proportional or fixed character printer.

A slight variation of the daisy wheel is the *thimble printer*. Its print element is cup or cylinder shaped rather than circular. The print characters are on the outside of the thimble and the hammer strikes the character from inside the cylinder.

The Dot Matrix Printer. Characters printed by a matrix printer consist of a series of dots, made by a block with protruding wires or pins. These pins act like little hammers that strike the ribbon against the page to create the characters. The resulting printed page can look very "computerized," and may not be suitable for formal business letters or printing a book. But they're fast and inexpensive. Matrix printers cost anywhere from $300 to $3,000, depending on the speed, the number of dots in the matrix, and the number of columns it prints. Speeds range from 50 to 600 characters per second. That's 500 to 6,000 words per minute.

Besides the advantage of its relatively low cost, a matrix printer can create different print sizes and styles, making the change of character size and style in mid-page an automatic function. No need to change print wheels in mid-page.

Newer models have *higher density print resolution*, meaning they use more dots to make the character. These machines use tricks like shifting the dots slightly and overstriking to generate higher quality print. Get a demonstration of one of these printers. They are more flexible and faster than the letter quality printers and a lot less expensive. I have seen printed sheets from matrix printers (including the one I own) that look like they were printed on a daisy wheel.

Thermal Printers

These are my last choice for word processing printers. Thermal printers are matrix printers which use heat printing techniques to create the characters. These printers are very inexpensive and quiet, but they require special paper which costs about five times more than normal paper and the paper has a tendency to darken with time.

Phototypesetting

A *phototypesetter* makes a photographic image of what's typed on the keyboard. These machines function like very sophisticated word processors that have numerous type sizes and styles on line (that is, available for use). The page of text is created either by projecting the characters directly onto photographic paper or by photographing the text from a high resolution video display screen.

Either way, you get high quality output on photographic paper which can then be pasted up for high volume offset printing.

The phototypesetter can be used on a stand-alone basis or as a very sophisticated word processor. Better yet, the text entered into your word processor can be sent to a phototypesetting machine through a link from your machine. This linked process saves the time of retyping the complete manuscript and leaves only the font selection controls to be entered into the text. Services are springing up that will take a manuscript from your word processor's memory and print it on a phototypesetter. More on this in Chapter 15.

Keyboards

In Chapter 3, I described a keyboard that contained an entire series of function keys to make editing easier. All machines designed specifically for word processing use similar keyboards. But you can also do word processing on a standard computer keyboard; it's just not as easy.

With a standard keyboard, all of the editing functions require that you press at least two keys. The standard computer keyboard has a second shift key called the CONTROL key. When this key is pressed at the same time as a normal key, the normal key is normal no longer. It is changed into a *function key*. For example, pressing the CONTROL and G keys together establishes the delete function; CONTROL and V is insert. Being a master of the understatement, let me say it's less convenient than the word processor keyboard and takes longer to learn. Do not purchase a machine with a keyboard that doesn't contain four separate cursor control keys, because you'll go bananas trying to control the cursor's movement with multiple keystrokes.

There are people who claim that multiple key entry systems are faster to use once the control codes are learned because your fingers never have to leave the home row. Others disagree. Happily, this debate is on its way out because the newer computers and video display terminals have what are called *programmable keys*. The keyboard has about ten extra keys that can become anything you want them to be—well, almost anything. Clever use of these keys can turn your computer into an extended keyboard word processor, giving you the best of both worlds.

I've already mentioned the convenience of a moveable keyboard, *i.e.*, one attached to the computer by a flexible cable so you can type from a position that suits your fancy. Personally, I would go crazy typing without one. But then, I'm 6'4" and don't fit into most chairs and desks comfortably.

Video Display Monitors

Monitors, or display screens, come in a wide variety of sizes and shapes, like TV sets, but are more reliable. A major consideration in selecting a word processor or computer is how many characters it can show on the screen window at one time. That's right, it's the computer or video display terminal that controls the number of characters on the screen and not the video monitor. The standard screen output is 80 characters (columns) across by 24 lines down. Because a normal page holds 85 characters across by 66 lines down, the display screen generally shows less than half a page at a time. Usually this is not a problem because scrolling will let you see all of the material on a page.

Some word processor manufacturers are now selling full-page screens or screens displaying two full pages at a time. There's even one manufacturer selling a full-page display that rotates onto its side creating a wide page for accounting sheets. Another manufacturer has a screen that displays half a page until you press a key that turns it into a full-page display. Although the full-page characters are too small for easy reading, it's useful for judging the general appearance of a page. Anything but the standard 80-character by 24-line display will cost extra. So, if you're not typing a lot of tables or work that requires a full-page display feature, stick with a 24-line screen.

Screen sizes range from 7-inch to 19-inch (diagonal), and usually display characters in white, green or amber on a black background. You can, however, find them with black letters on a white background, like a typed piece of paper—but the easiest on your eyes is green on a black background. Adjustable and glare reduction screens are designed to stop distracting reflections (the type that bug you when you're trying to watch television in a brightly lit room). An adjustable screen allows you to position it for more comfortable viewing.

If you go the personal computer route, there is a good chance you can turn a used black and white TV into a CRT with the purchase of a low-cost *RF adapter*. This adapter converts the computer video signal into a signal that enters the TV through its antenna wires. The only problem with this approach is that there is a significant reduction in display quality, and a poor display can ruin your eyes. Imagine trying to read a page of type through a TV snowstorm.

The characters on the screen are made up of dots in a pattern—a dot matrix. Different machines use differing numbers of dots in the matrix (they range from 5x7 to 9x24 blocks of dots). The major difference is the crispness of the displayed character: how easy it is for you to read. The lower resolution displays do not have lowercase descenders on the characters like y, j, g, etc. These characters appear on the line instead of descending below it, making them more difficult to read.

Make sure the unit you choose is easy to read. You'll be looking at it for a long time. The easiest way to check the character quality is to compare the following characters on the screen : R & B, X & K, Q & O, S & 5, U & V. How easily can you tell the difference? Now look at the letters with descenders: y, j, p & q. Are they easy to read? Adjust the brightness and contrast on the CRT to see how the characters change. Do they get blurred and go out of focus? Is the cursor clearly indicated? How is the highlighting? Study all of these features carefully—it's your eyes that are at stake!

We've got it. You're looking at Database

11
Selecting a System

When you go looking for a word processing system, your biggest consideration should be that its parts are well integrated for the functions you want it to perform. It should be easy to learn how to use, responsive to your commands, and enable you to write, edit, and file simply and quickly. So how do you go about selecting the one system for you from the hundreds out there?

The Checklists

For help with the selection of a system to support your particular writing needs, turn to Appendix II and look at the checklists. They list all the available word processor software and hardware features. Go through the list and check off the features that are vital for the type of work you'll be doing. The checklists are an important tool to help you determine what features you will really need.

Take the list with you when you go to speak with salespeople. They will show you systems with lots of features and it's easy to lose track of which system has what. Filling out the list, feature by feature, for each system will enable you to make direct comparisons of all the systems you have looked at.

The First Stop

No matter how small your budget, start by looking at the best and most expensive word processing systems available—the stand-alone (the everything-you-could-ever-want) machines. These systems, designed specifically for word processing, offer convenient features like extended keyboards, full-page screens, and efficient, flexible editing software.

You're probably asking, "Why look at the luxury models when all I can afford is an economy model?" Here's why: to establish a standard for comparison with less costly and less sophisticated machines. It'll let you know very clearly what you're getting and not getting for your money. In Appendix III I've listed the names and addresses of companies which sell highly rated stand-alone word processors. Check your phone directory, find the local dealership, and call for a demonstration. Don't be overwhelmed by the price. Pretend you are John D. Rockefeller and have money to burn.

At the showroom, start by looking at the instruction manuals for the stand-alone machines. Pick out one that seems easy to follow. Sit down and feel how responsive the keys are to your touch. Check the number, functions and arrangement of the special keys. Take out your worksheet and talk to the salesperson about file storage, the software, the operating system, and all the features you've checked as being important to you. What about the printer? Does it do what you need it to do? Letter quality printing? Proportional printing? Can the system be easily upgraded to do jobs other than word processing? What other software is available? Can it talk to other machines? Does it use a standard operating system?

Don't be intimidated by the language salespeople use. Those who really understand the systems should have no difficulty explaining the terminology and operations in simple terms. Computers and word processors are changing so rapidly that there's frequently not enough time to train all the salespeople adequately on every system. But make sure that all your questions on the checklist get answered and write down all the responses.

After playing Rockefeller at the stand-alone showroom, look at the compact models, and then at the low-cost economy models. These will usually be found at your local computer distributors and stores and sold as personal computers. Start with the Resource Appendix. See the full sprectrum of what's available. Continue to fill out the worksheet until you have writer's cramp. If you follow this procedure, whether you choose a stand-alone or a cheapie computer with a TV set, you'll be satisfied with it and you'll know the reason why.

Talk to the Users

When talking with a salesperson, ask for the names of companies or individuals who have the system you think you might want. Call them and find out what they like least and most about it. What things drive them crazy? Which features are they addicted to?

User Groups

Virtually every computer and word processor brand has a "user group" or club associated with it. Don't misunderstand what they're about; they were not formed by the companies as a scheme to sell more systems, but by users as a way to share information about their systems. These users probably know more about the subtleties of operating the systems than the manufacturer does. However, they tend to be biased toward *their* brand of machine and will tell you everything wrong with other systems. But they are an enthusiastic and helpful group of people, and probably can arrange a demo on one of their systems.

Finding Data and Evaluations

Data Pro is a name to remember. They publish evaluations and guides for the computer industry, and report equipment evaluations made by system owners. They have a complete index and comparison charts of all the available word processing equipment available. The only drawback is that the two enormous volumes of The *Data Pro Word Processing Series* cost several hundred dollars a year. For that price, you also get to ask Data Pro's technical consultants questions about any phase of system selection or operation. On the other hand, most univeristy libraries have copies of the Data Pro series in their reference sections which you can look at for free. Just bring your lunch and don't make any other appointments for the day. I find their glossary of terms, manufacturer listings and up-to-date comparison charts invaluable.

Other Sources of Information

If you want to try out some word processors and computers without tramping from store to store, attend a small computer or word processing trade show. Usually held in large urban areas, their purpose is to sell equipment and provide a forum for sharing information. Vendors of all brands of equipment gather at these shows to ply their wares. It's like a carnival side show, each booth claiming to offer something better than the next. This is not a place to reflect on anything, much less the merits of one machine over another. But it's an opportunity to try out some equipment and, if you are lucky, you might get invited to one of the raucous after-hours cocktail parties.

Local distributors and computer store area vendors often give out free passes to these shows (the exhibitions, not the cocktail parties). But if you can't wrangle a free pass, the entrance fee for the equipment exhibition is never more than $5.

What Next?

After you have gone through the above procedures, you'll have a good idea which systems can do the job for you. By now you know which features you can't live without, and what price you're willing to pay for them. If you're like me, you'll wake up one morning with the name and model number of a particular brand humming in your brain and want to rush out to buy it. But don't, not until you've read the next chapter on getting a system.

12
Financial Arrangements: The Economics of It All

By now you're probably ready to run down to your local computer store, plunk down your money, and carry your system home. Well, don't! Not, at least, until you've read this chapter. I'll give you some info to make your purchase a little easier and maybe even save you some money.

Once you've chosen your word proces sor, the next step is figuring out the best deal. Such as, should you purchase, lease or rent? Let's look at the advantages and disadvantages of each. Then I'll tell you what to look for in the fine print of the contract you'll be signing.

Purchasing

Purchasing your system offers numerous tax advantages if you have a small business or are self-employed. It qualifies you for an investment tax credit. In addition, if you borrow to finance the purchase you can deduct interest payments from your taxable income. No only that, but the total value of the equipment can be depreciated over a three to five year period. Tax laws keep changing, so check with an accountant or one of the tax guides to figure how much you can save.

On the other hand, there are some disadvantages to buying a word processor. First, word processor and computer technology is rapidly improving, so you risk being stuck owning an old-fashioned, obsolete model. Top of the line word processors of two years ago are really primitive compared to even today's low-cost systems. And there's no reason to expect this trend to change. Second, if you're not absolutely sure what type of system you'll ultimately need, you could find yourself stuck with an inappropriate machine. Third, because the price of computer equipment keeps dropping you will find that whatever you buy today will be available tomorrow at a much lower price. (Computer technology is one of the few commodities that keeps ahead of the inflation rate.) Fourth, unless you borrow the funds, you'll have to tie up capital in the purchase. But, compared with the high cost of renting, the tax advantages of buying make it an attractive option.

Leasing

Leasing may appear to be the best of all worlds. You won't have to tie up much cash, because leasing requires prepayment of only a few monthly installments. Leases usually run from three to five years, with an option to purchase the equipment at an additional cost at the end of the term. This gives you the advantage of buying through installments, with the last payment five years down the line, all at today's prices. The disadvantages are: the machine winds up costing more than if you bought it outright and, as I mentioned earlier, the price of computer equipment keeps dropping. Also, leases are extremely difficult to get out of, and "full payment leases" pretty much guarantee the lessor a substantial profit and the tax advantages of equipment ownership as well. The lease may or may not include a maintenance contract. It's important to check this out because maintenance can cost a bundle.

From a tax perspective several leasing options are possible. The lease may be considered either a true lease or a conditional sale. Under the terms of a conditional sale, part of the monthly payments can be deducted as interest, and because the conditional sale eventually results in ownership, the investment tax credit and depreciation benefits are also available. Under a straight lease arrangement, the company leasing you the equipment maintains ownership and receives the tax break, which may or may not be passed on to you under the terms of the lease. Leasing would be advantageous to smaller companies or individuals who are not making enough money to require a tax shelter or who might have difficulty obtaining financing for the purchase of a word processor.

Renting

When you lease or purchase you're making a long-term commitment to a particular piece of equipment. If you rent, on the other hand, you'll have time to try out a system or to complete a crucial project on a short-term basis, Renting costs much more in the long run than buying or leasing, but you can deduct these costs from your taxes if you're using the word processor for business.

Beware! If you decide to rent, pay close attention to the length of the rental period and the amount of notice you must give to terminate the contract. Some rental agreements are automatically renewed if you move like a turtle and are too slow in notifying the company of your intention to terminate.

Buying and Selling Used Equipment

Look in the classified section of any large urban newspaper for listings of personal or small business computers and word processors, and you'll see that a vast market has been developing for the purchase and sale of used computer equipment. Many of these ads, unhappily, are placed by people who did not read this book and purchased the wrong equipment for their word processing needs. But many older or used systems which have been replaced by newer and faster models still work well because the electronic portions of the system have no moving parts to wear out. They can be excellent buys. I have seen current model, used machines being sold for 50 to 70 percent of their new price.

If the classifieds don't have what you've been looking for, there may be an organization in your area which brings prospective buyers and sellers together for a modest fee; a sort of computer matchmaker. Before buying a used system it's important to check if the machine is still being serviced and supported by the manufacturer. If not, don't buy it!

Because of the money I save, I always wind up buying used computers. But then, that's my style. I purchase most of my things used. The classified ads are my favorite section of the newspaper. However, to purchase used equipment you must have ready cash. You may have trouble trying to convince a bank to lend you money for a used computer advertised in the paper. Banks don't accept personal computers as collateral yet.

Contracts

Buying or leasing a word processor can be a lot more complicated than buying or leasing a TV or microwave oven. I suggest that you sign a contract with the vendor. Now I'll tell you what makes a good contract.

A successful contract is one that no one ever bothers to look at after it is signed. It just gathers dust in some drawer because each of the parties is in complete agreement about their mutual responsibilities. An unsuccessful contract, on the other hand, leaves at least one of the parties constantly reading and rereading it, quoting sections as a threat to the other. Not too much fun.

Computer and word processing vendors have extremely well-written standard sales contracts for hardware and software. But because *their* lawyers write the contract, it protects them and doesn't offer you a thing in the way of protection. Show this contract to your lawyer before signing it! A lawyer's fee is an inexpensive insurance policy for the money you're going to lay out. I suggest adding some of the items listed below to the contract before you buy—not only for your legal protection, but as a sincerity test for the vendor. If all the vendor's promises and claims are true, he or she should not object to putting them in writing. Still, quite a few vendors do refuse to put their promises in writing. If this happens, look elsewhere for your machine!

The following things should definitely be discussed with the salespeople. Try to get them to agree in writing to as many of them as possible. Unless you're a whiz at negotiating you probably won't get everything you want. But the process should help you clarify exactly what you'll be getting when you buy the system. In other words, it is a way of assuring that you and the vendor are on the same wavelength.

Specifications

The system specification section of the contract should contain a list of:

1) All the physical equipment (hardware) you'll be purchasing, including a detailed description of each part with it's model number. And don't forget the connecting cables.

2) A list of all software, including *version number* to be supplied and your rights regarding their use. (See Chapter 7 on software licenses.)

3) The storage capacities for the machine's memory and disk drives.

4) All manuals to be supplied with the system as well as any educational materials or classes to be provided.

If you can, include the promised upgrade possibilities, such as being able to support more than one word processing station, and the cost of each upgrade. Then, and this is very important, include a list of the functions you expect the word processor to perform. For instance, if you were told the word processor would automatically backup your files, include that in the contract. You want to avoid buying a system you've been promised has certain capabilities and then find you have to spend more money on additional equipment or software to get it to perform those functions.

If possible, insert a clause stating that you have relied on the vendor's expertise in purchasing your system. This could afford you additional protection if your purchase turns out to be a complete disaster.

Payment Terms

If you are purchasing, be sure your contract states the *total purchase price* of the system. This price should include the costs of hardware, software, installation and financing. Before signing, be sure that you and the vendor arc in agreement that there will be no additional costs over what's stated in the contract.

If you've decided to lease the system make sure the contract clearly states the following:

1) Payment due dates and late payment penalty charges.

2) Cancellation notice requirements and penalties.

3) Clearly defined purchase provisions for the end of the lease period.

4) Who owns the hardware and software.

5) If possible, provisions for costs and options to upgrade the system to a more advanced model during the lease period.

Maintenance and Warranty

Here's where you have to polish your magnifying glass. Whatever it takes, please read the warranty carefully! The warranty period for a word processor is usually 90 days and covers complete replacement or repair of any malfunctions during that period.

In addition to the warranty, the contract should clearly spell out who will be responsible for repairs after the warranty period is up. Also, what is the expected turn-around time for repairs? It's frustrating to be forced to wait while parts for your machine are being shipped across the country.

A year's maintenance contract typically costs about 12 percent of the total hardware cost. It should specify whether the technician makes house calls or if you must haul the equipment back to the shop for repairs. Most maintenance contracts provide a replacement machine so you won't be without a working system for more than two days.

The contract should also cover software maintenance and the cost of updates. Most popular software packages don't have many problems because all the bugs have been worked out by hundreds of users. But problems do occur, and you should protect yourself against the possibility. Also, check the cost associated with software improvements or upgrades to your system.

Delivery and Installation

Your contract should contain the delivery and installation dates and specify that, before the final payment is made, a series of tests will be run to make sure that the equipment is operating correctly. Smaller systems are usually tested by the retailer at the store. Make it a point to be present during the testing, and you'll get a free lesson in how to set up and operate your machine. If you can't be there, at least get the salesperson to show you how to set it up yourself.

Larger systems are usually installed and tested at your office. Make sure that the contract clearly states this, and specify that you want the system to be working without a hitch before the installation person gets away.

Disclaimer

I included this section on contracts merely as a guide. Don't use it in place of advice from a lawyer. Contracts must include items like legal recourse, liability sections and other things that only lawyers are qualified to deal with. So have a lawyer go over the contract before you sign it. Then you both can check the fine print and add some of your own terms to protect your investment. In other words, make sure you cover your assets!

Insurance

Those of you who work at home might find that your standard household insurance policy does not cover a computer used for business. In addition, many business policies consider a computer to be a fancy typewriter. Check what your policy does and does not cover. Computer insurance policies are available for $100-$200 per year and will protect you and your machine from problems caused by accident, theft or vandalism. Make sure that your software is also covered by the policy.

There is a policy that will insure you against the accidental erasure of data or text files.

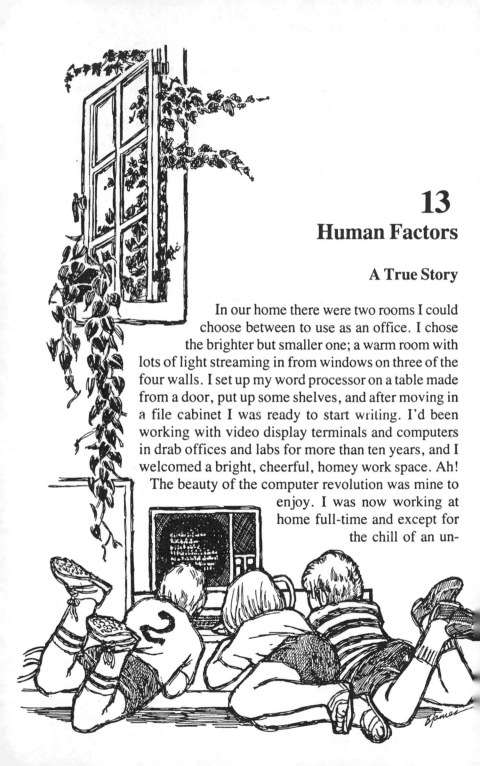

13
Human Factors

A True Story

In our home there were two rooms I could choose between to use as an office. I chose the brighter but smaller one; a warm room with lots of light streaming in from windows on three of the four walls. I set up my word processor on a table made from a door, put up some shelves, and after moving in a file cabinet I was ready to start writing. I'd been working with video display terminals and computers in drab offices and labs for more than ten years, and I welcomed a bright, cheerful, homey work space. Ah! The beauty of the computer revolution was mine to enjoy. I was now working at home full-time and except for the chill of an unusually cold winter, the first six months of research and writing went fine. My inexpensive microcomputer left a lot to be desired in the way of slick functions, but together we proved that a cheapo word processor could easily handle the first draft of a book. By spring I had bought a more sophisticated system and was spending long hours at a time revising the manuscript. After several days of intense work, I started getting headaches in the afternoon. That was a new one for me; I never get headaches. Because they happened in the afternoon, I assumed they were caused by intense work and hunger. But then it became increasingly difficult to get up in the morning. My eyes ached the way they do when I've only had two hours of sleep. It seemed they were always tired. Suddenly it dawned on me that I was suffering from a *terminal* disease! This book and my machine were wiping me out.

What a dilemma! My book would encourage people to enter the computer revolution, even though I knew that working with computers could mess up their bodies. Do I continue or should I just call the project off and let someone else be the Pied Piper of word processing?

I started collecting information on health problems associated with video display terminals. It didn't take long for me to find out that I wasn't the only one experiencing eye and muscle problems from working on a word processor. In 1981, the American Newspaper Guild, a labor organization representing newspaper workers, released an alarming report stating that more than 60 percent of its union members complained of eye problems, backache and muscle strain from working on CRTs. Due to the severity of the complaints in this report, the National Institute for Occupational Safety and Health (NIOSH) conducted an extensive study in San Francisco, which led it to issue safety recommendations for workers using video display terminals. Currently the Newspaper Guild and the AFL-CIO are trying to establish equipment and work guidelines for all union contracts. Working Woman, a national organization, set up an extensive research program on office health hazards and has become a clearing house for information. I have listed references to all of these studies in Appendix III.

Researching and writing this chapter has taken more time than the rest of the book, and I hope you'll spend a lot of time studying it. Pay heed to the recommendations. The first one is: Don't work on a word processor for extended periods of time until you read the rest of this chapter.

Ergonomics

Ergonomics is a field of study devoted to the working relationship between people and machines. It looks at the design of machines and the workspaces in which they're used, to promote human safety, comfort and productivity. Ergonomics for the office environment reached prominence in Europe where labor unions set guidelines for equipment to be used by clerical workers. They also established standards for furniture design, lighting requirements and work load, which are actually enforced by law in several countries.

These regulations made it illegal for many European companies to use some American-made word processing and video display terminals. So, to regain sales in the European market, several American manufacturers incorporated European design guidelines into their product line. After ergonomically-designed, American-made machines began selling in Europe, it became obvious to those manufacturers that if they were selling safer equipment in other countries they should do the same at home. That's how ergonomically-designed equipment came to the U.S., and with it an attitude that the people operating machines are more important than the machines.

What Are the Health Problems?

There's some concern that low level radiation given off by VDTs and television sets might cause cancer and cataracts and could be responsible for birth defects. If you are pregnant or plan to become pregnant, check the latest information *before* operating a word processor or computer. No cause-and-effect relationship has been proven yet—but would you really want to take the chance.?

The National Institute of Occupational Safety and Health (NIOSH) keeps a file of radiation-related reports and has begun a two-year study to compare the pregnancies of VDT users with those of non-users. Contact NIOSH and Working Woman at the addresses listed in the Health Factors Resource List in Appendix III.

Numerous studies are underway on all facets of computer and CRT use, but the major difficulties uncovered so far are the ones that affected me: eye strain, headaches, and body ache. None of the studies I have read so far advise against using word processors. However, here is what they do advocate:

1. All word processing equipment should be designed to meet ergonomic standards.

2. Lighting and other office environmental factors should be properly adjusted.

3. Office furniture used for word processing should be constructed to accommodate the people using it.

4. Proper operating and work procedures should be established.

I'll elaborate on these four points to help you create a safe work environment and establishing procedures to ease the strain on your eyes, head and muscles. Word processors are not dangerous if they are used properly and located in an adequately designed environment.

The main CRT-related *eye* problems are: soreness, stinging, burning, itching, blurred vision, and dull headaches. Eye strain symptoms have been linked to either faulty lighting or improperly designed equipment.

Now for a mini eye anatomy lesson. There are basically three muscles in the eye that can be overworked and strained: the *oculomotor muscles* which move the eye from side to side, the *iris muscle* which adjusts the size of the pupil to accom- 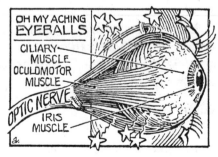 modate varying light intensities, and the *ciliary muscles* which change the shape of the eye lens to bring objects into focus. Most eye problems are caused by overworking the iris and ciliary muscles.

When you focus at close range, as when reading from a CRT, the ciliary muscles must keep the eye lens constantly compressed.

That's why working at close range for long periods of time tires the eyes. The iris muscles become overworked when the pupil is forced to open and close frequently to adjust between the low light levels on the CRT screen and the brightness in the surrounding room. The strain on both muscles can be minimized by workng in an environment with properly designed lighting, and by taking adequate rest breaks.

Lighting Quality

Correct office lighting requires consideration of both the quality and quantity of light in the workspace. You want lighting fixtures that create indirect, reflected or shielded light. The best light is reflected from ceilings and walls, rather than direct lighting. A direct light source in your field of vision can cause headaches as a result of overworked iris muscles. Use the illustration as a guide for establishing proper light quality your word processor station.

Believe it or not, fluorescent lighting is easier on your eyes than incandescent lighting. But in a room where the light is relatively subdued, incandescent lights may be mixed with "warm" type fluorescent lamps. If your office lighting is a mixture of artificial and day light, use a "white" type fluorescent lamp. There is also a "universal" fluorescent tube which mixes well with both daylight and incandescent lighting.

If your word processor will be used in a room with windows, choose a northern exposure since northern light is steady and soft. Eastern exposure is the next best, followed by southern and then western.

Light Levels

Traditional office lighting design is based on the premise of the more light the better; standards always specify minimum allowable lighting levels. Putting a CRT into a business or home office changes all of this.

Characters on a word processor screen are formed from minute dots of low intensity light on a dark background. The screen image can be overpowered by reflections of objects in the room, including your own

LIGHT SOURCES

GOOD

INDIRECT

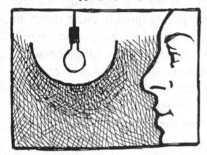

DIFFUSE

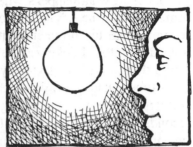

POOR

DIRECT GLARE

REFLECTED GLARE

DIRECTED TOWARDS EYE

TOO SUBDUED

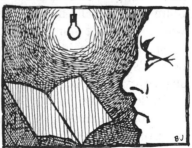

image, if normal office level lighting is used. The brighter the lighting in the room, the more intense the reflective glare on the screen. Screen glare will cause you to strain while reading the screen text, or to shift position continually to read parts of the screen. Another problem created by too much light in the room is analogous to what happens when you leave a movie theater and come out into the daylight. Your pupils quickly close down to accommodate the brighter light, and during that period there's some discomfort. Looking at the dark screen of a word processor in a brightly lit room forces your eyes to go through the same motions every time you look away from the screen. This could mean the iris muscles are opening and closing the pupils of your eyes every few seconds. Bright light reflected from the walls in front and to the side of the word processor screen can create large contrast ranges in your field of vision, further aggravating the problem.

It might seem that the way to stop eye strain is to reduce the light level until you're working in a nearly dark room. This won't work, because you must also read printed material while using the word processor. The solution is to reduce the light level to a point where both reflective and direct glare are eliminated, while making sure there's still enough light to read printed or written material. Lighting experts recommend a light level slightly less than half that of a typical office.

The illumination or overall light level is measured in terms of *foot candles:* the amount of light one foot from a standard light source. The recommended illumination level for an office is 100-200 foot-candles. If a video display terminal is being used, the illumination should be in the range of 35-70 foot-candles. If you want to check the illumination level in your office, the local electric company can provide a lighting engineer to measure it. (Please note: it's impossible to determine light levels with your naked eye since eyes automatically adjust to changes in illumination level.)

While illumination level (foot-candles) is the overall light level in the room, *luminance* is the measure of light reflected towards the eye from a surface. Ergonomists say that when you're working on a word processor, all surfaces (desk, walls, keyboard, etc.) within your field of vision should have a luminance level no greater than three times that of the display screen. And the luminance of the walls and other surfaces within your peripheral vision are to be no brighter than eight to ten times the screen luminance.

A Handy Do-It-Yourself Test. When I was trying to straighten out the lighting in my office, I discovered a way to measure the luminance level in the room using my inexpensive 35mm camera

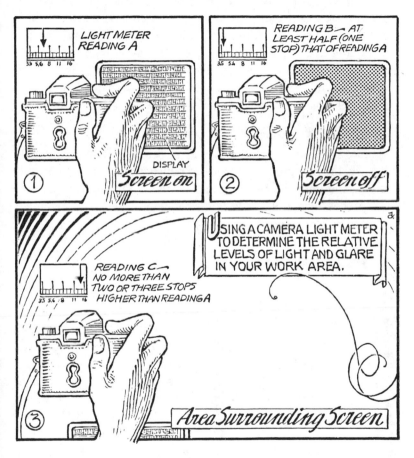

light meter. The accompanying illustration shows how my camera technique works. This simple procedure lets you check and adjust environmental lighting to minimize conditions that lead to iris muscle fatigue.

You can also use the camera light meter to measure the amount of reflective glare on a CRT screen. First take a light reading with the screen totally dark, then a second reading with textual material on the screen. If the second reading is less than twice that of the dark screen, you've got excessive reflective glare. So read on.

Manufacturers can reduce reflective glare by applying a non-glare coating to the CRT screen. Systems with non-glare screens are definitely worth the small additional expense. If your display doesn't have a non-glare screen, you can purchase a filter to place in front of the screen. Although it cuts down brightness considerably, I advise using a Polaroid filter. Steer away from the colored plastic panels and etched faceplates which not only reduce image brightness but also reduce image clarity. Adjustable or tiltable display screens can be positioned to reduce reflective glare.

The Solution to the Lighting Problem

There are three factors involved in setting office lighting for CRT use: the amount and location of both natural and artificial light sources, the intensity of the screen image, and the position of the word processor in relation to lights and windows.

I hit upon this solution to my lighting problems. I realized that if I

worked on the word processor while facing a window, the bright daylight created a direct glare problem. On the other hand, if I worked with a window directly behind me, it created reflective glare. So I moved my desk to face a wall between two windows, with the only windowless wall to my back. Voila, no glare! I then put bottom-up shades on all the windows I chose bottom-up shades so I could have a source of daylight in the room above my field of vision. I installed a fluorescent fixture on the ceiling and a small adjustable desk lamp for reading written or printed copy. The room doesn't look as homey as it did before, but my eyes sure feel a lot better.

I'm the only one working in my room, so I get to play boss and have complete say on the lighting and furniture arrangement. Those of you working in an office with other people don't have as much freedom. But if headaches, eye strain, or camera light meter readings indicate the room lighting is not suited for word processing, it's time to make some changes. If the other people in your office need brighter light, then install partitions to reduce the light level near the word processor. If direct or indirect glare is a problem, then hang curtains on the windows or move the machine. If the lighting is too bright, see if electrical dimmers can be attached—or, as a last resort, remove some of the bulbs. Don't use sunglasses! They can cause a whole series of other eye problems.

In the hardware chapter I spoke about CRT character resolution and screen intensity. Double check that your screen has crisp readable letters that are easily adjusted for contrast and brightness. A crisp, bright image reduces eye strain, as does a green-on-black or yellow on amber screen. Black letters on a white screen are great for reducing glare, but they have been known to have a flicker effect. This can cause more damage than glare problems. Glare can also be caused by reflections off bright surfaces such as chrome around the office or shiny keyboard keys.

Details on the ergonomic factors of equipment design can be found in the *VDT Manual* listed in the reference section. For the most part, go with your own judgement as to what feels comfortable for you. Looking at several available systems will give you insight into which features are best for your work habits.

Muscle Problems

Place your word processor screen and keyboard in a comfortable working position. This is easy to do if your word processor has a moveable screen and keyboard, and if your office has adjustable furniture. Ergonomic design factors require the keyboard to be

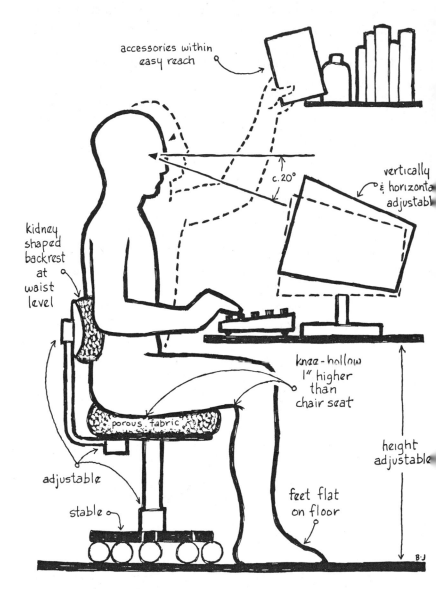

accessories within easy reach

c. 20°

vertically & horizontal adjustabl

kidney shaped backrest at waist level

knee-hollow 1" higher than chair seat

porous fabric

height adjustable

adjustable

stable

feet flat on floor

B·J

PROPER POSTURE & EQUIPMENT

attached to the system by a cable at least three feet long and the screen to be adjustable both horizontally and vertically (swivel and tilt). If your word processor does not have these features, you're more likely to suffer from body aches.

Furniture

It's important that your chair and word processor be placed to accomodate your body. So, if you don't already have coordinated and comfortable furniture, then buy or build some. You'll definitely need adjustable furniture if more than one person will be using the equipment.

The Chair. Adjust the height of your chair seat so that, when you sit with your feet flat on the floor and your knees bent at a 90 degree angle, the distance from the hollow of your knee to the floor is one inch higher than the seat. This inch prevents pressure from being put on your thigh, constraining blood flow. The chair bottom should be horizontal, slightly concave and made of a porous material to let air circulate. So avoid solid plastic or wooden chairs.

You should be able to adjust your chair while sitting on it. Some newer office chairs have hydraulic lifting mechanisms that are a real snap to adjust. The chair's backrest should adjust both horizontally and vertically. Did you know that it's not your back that needs support, but your pelvis? Make sure the backrest is positioned to provide support at your waist level. The chair should swivel and lock into position. The European standards call for the chair to have five casters if it's on wheels because of the stability offered by the fifth wheel. I also recommend armrests for those long work sessions.

The Desk. The best desk height places the keyboard so your elbow is bent at about 90 degrees when you're typing. This means the desk height must be set relative to the chair height. The desk surface should be a matte finish so it doesn't become a source of reflective glare. You need sufficient leg room to sit comfortably, and a large enough work surface to hold the machine, lamps, paper, jelly beans, and other important materials. If more than one person will be using the system, the shorter people may need an adjustable foot rest.

Sitting at the Terminal. The accompanying illustration shows the ideal physical arrangement between you and your machine. It's easily established if your chair and desk are adjustable. Your head will feel best tilted forward about 20 degrees, spine arched forward slightly when viewed from the side. Your upper arms should be vertical and you shouldn't have to twist your head or torso. Keep your thighs approximately horizontal, and the lower part of your legs approximately vertical. Keep all supplies easily accessible and organized according to frequency of use.

Document Holders. The most highly stressed part of the body (besides the brain) is your neck. To reduce neck strain use an adjustable document holder for keeping your draft copy or worksheet in an easily viewable position. The *worst* place for these papers is on the desk surface alongside the keyboard. Documents placed on the desk surface—besides being a literal pain in the neck—become a glare source by reflecting overhead light.

ADJUSTABLE FURNITURE

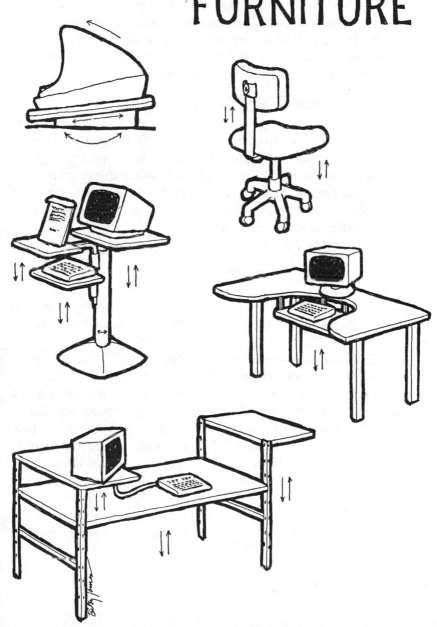

The document holder should be adjustable and have a place marker. Position the holder so it's roughly the same distance from your eye as the screen, minimizing the amount of refocusing required as you scan back and forth between the two.

Note: Under all circumstances *avoid* document holders that use a magnet to attach the written copy to the holder surface. As previously mentioned in the files chapter, magnets can do irreparable damage to material stored on floppy disks.

The Well Designed Work Area

The accompanying illustration shows some adjustable furniture design ideas for word processor work areas. Building or purchasing a small, adjustable word processor work station will give you lighting control as well as the ability to establish a comfortable position.

Because printer noises are very loud and can be annoying and distracting, I recommend installing either a *printer sound shield* or an acoustic enclosure on the printer.

Be Good to Yourself

One of the first things to do if you will be working on a word processor is to have your eyes examined. It's a good idea to schedule regular appointments every six to twelve months to check for vision problems. Many trade unions are negotiating annual eye examinations into CRT and word processor operator contracts.

To prevent eye focus and back muscle problems, take a 10-15 minute break after every hour of work on a word processor. Get up and move away from the word processor, preferably to a space where you can look at distant objects. It's also a good idea to rotate your work tasks to break up word processing sessions into shorter periods. As with any type of desk work, stretching exercises at break time will make your muscles feel great. You can usually find a place like a hallway or the parking lot where you can do them. Try to limit your daily work time at the word processor to no more than five hours a day—with five breaks. Sound good?

14
Setting Things Up

Like a new baby, a word processing system requires special supplies, certain environmental conditions and operating procedures. This chapter will tell you how to set up and keep your word processor humming along.

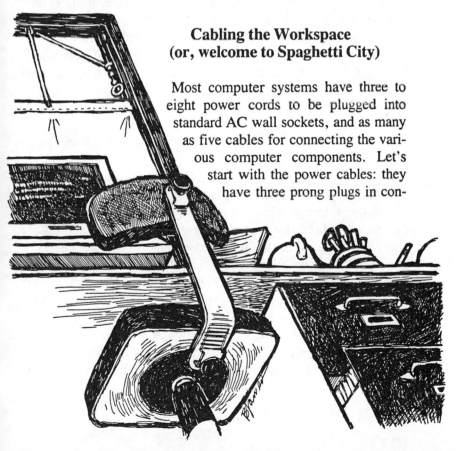

Cabling the Workspace
(or, welcome to Spaghetti City)

Most computer systems have three to eight power cords to be plugged into standard AC wall sockets, and as many as five cables for connecting the various computer components. Let's start with the power cables: they have three prong plugs in contrast to the household appliance's two-pronged type. Why the third prong? It's a ground wire whose primary purpose is to prevent electrical shocks. In simple terms, the ground wire provides a return circuit (in place of you) in case a live wire touches the case. It also reduces the chance of stray electric currents interfering with your machine's operation.

If your electrical outlets are the two-prong type, you can purchase adapters at any hardware store to convert them to the three-wire variety. You attach the hanging wire on these gizmos to an adequate ground line, which in most cases is merely the screw on the faceplate of the outlet. If you're unsure about the ground attachment, get a friend with a test meter or an electrician to test the ground connection for you. While you're checking outlets, let me warn you that, if your system components are wired to more than one outlet and the wiring of one of the outlets is reversed, you can do incredible damage to your machines. So make sure all outlets are wired according to standards. I prefer plugging my power cords into a junction box which has four to six outlets and only one cord that's plugged into the wall. The junction box provides a neat, convenient way to plug in my word processor, printer, and anything else requiring electrical power.

If all the components in your system are built into one unit, then you'll have only the printer cable to attach. The rest of us will have cables connecting the disk drives (floppy or hard), the keyboard, monitor and printer. The disk drives are connected by what's called a *ribbon connector*, while the monitor and keyboard are attached by relatively thin circular cables. By the way, it's important to attach the clips and screws provided with most computer cables.

Make sure all cables are routed behind the unit, out of the way of your actual work area. If you decide to locate your printer away from the actual word processor, route its cable through the ceiling, or use a plastic-sectioned bridge cover if it must be on the floor. With as many as 13 wires routed through your workspace, you must plan their route to prevent someone from tripping over them and hurting themselves, or perhaps even knocking the whole machine onto the floor.

Power Considerations

The standard voltage in an electrical outlet is from 110 to 130 volts, and is called 120 volts. For those of you who are not familiar with the term volts, suffice it to say that the higher the voltage the greater the potential for electricity to flow. In commercial installations, power to a word processor is provided by a *dedicated circuit,* a wire or cable that connects the wall socket directly to the fuse box. In my house it wasn't possible to run a dedicated line to my work room. So I checked what other outlets and lights were on the same line as the computer socket. I did this by turning off the circuit breaker for my work room and going around the house to see what other appliances and lights were turned off by my flicking that switch. I found that the living room outlets were on the same circuit. So, I make sure no one ever uses the vacuum cleaner in the living room while I am working on my machine. Why? Well, an appliance like a vacuum cleaner or air conditioner requires a lot of current to run. The effect of turning on a high current appliance is a slight drop in the voltage on its line. This slight voltage drop can cause the computer system's memory to be erased, exactly as if you had turned the power off. If this happens while you are in the middle of working on a long document you could lose what you have just typed in.

Even worse, and this is much less likely, the voltage drop can screw up a portion of the floppy in one of the drives if it occurs while the system is writing on a disk. I have worked on a machine in a house where a washing machine was on a completely separate circuit, and saw a computer fail when the washer was turned on. How do you know it's happening? Did you ever notice the lights dim in a room when you turned on an appliance? Well, that's it. The lights dim because the voltage drops. But, if you have to work in a place where someone could always turn on a washing machine or office copier, all is not lost. There are devices called *voltage regulators* that maintain a constant voltage independent of what else is being turned on. These devices cost about $300 and are easy to install. You plug the regulator into a grounded outlet and then plug your machine into an outlet on the side of the regulator. It will also protect your system against what is known as a "brown-out," the result of the power company sensing an overload condition and reducing the supply voltage. Call your local electric company to find out whether brown-outs are something to be concerned about where you live.

The voltage supplied to outlets will frequently show rapid, short duration fluctuations. Unfortunately, these voltage changes can do physical damage to the low-cost power supply that's in your small computer. A *line filter* will protect your machine from these power fluctuations. I purchased a junction box with six outlets and a built-in line filter for $55. I don't know if I really need it, but it was only a few dollars more than a plain junction box and I figured it was easily worth the price for my piece of mind.

If power in your area goes out relatively frequently and it's critical that you never lose information, consider installing an uninterruptable power supply. These devices use a battery and will keep your machine running for around ten minutes after the local power cuts out. This will give you enough time to store your work and shut down your system properly. They cost about $900. I think that's a lot of money to spend unless you have a multiple terminal system and critical information needs. Backup disks are sufficient insurance for most of us.

Static Electricity

I always think about static electricity when I'm in a carpeted hotel walking toward the elevator because, on many occasions, I've been zapped by a spark flying out from my finger as I reached for the elevator button. What makes this happen? On a dry day, walking several steps on a carpet can generate thousands of volts in your body. Touch the computer keyboard or the computer itself, and the static discharge could zap your machine, causing the loss of everything you've been typing or, even worse, damage a circuit component. Static discharges can jump from your body to a machine when you are standing as far as a foot away from the machine. Static discharges can also cause serious problems for floppy disks as well.

If the humidity in your area is over 50 percent, static electricity will not be a problem. If it's not, get a humidifier or, even better, get an *anti-static mat* for about $50 to place near the machine. These mats have metal fibers woven in them to discharge any static build-up as you walk on them.

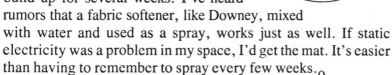

There are anti-static sprays, costing about $10 a can, that can be sprayed on the carpet to give protection from static build up for several weeks. I've heard rumors that a fabric softener, like Downey, mixed with water and used as a spray, works just as well. If static electricity was a problem in my space, I'd get the mat. It's easier than having to remember to spray every few weeks.

Air Conditioning

Dust, dirt and smoke in the air can play havoc with any computer. All three of these can wreck both floppy and hard disks, destroying not only the programs or text stored on them, but the disks themselves. Dirt and dust will eventually create problems for the moving parts in your printer and can cause many of the electrical components in the system to get hot. The higher the temperature of an electrical component, the shorter its life. Solutions: No Smoking signs in the vicinity of the machine will save the lives of your disks and friends. If dust and dirt are a problem in your locale, look into installing air conditioning.

Speaking of dirt, I always resist the temptation to place a coffee cup on the table that my word processor is on. Accidentally spilled liquids have done in a lot of systems.

If the room temperature is set for your comfort, the machine will be comfortable as well. If the machine gets too hot, you may encounter sporadic memory failure or disk read errors. From 55°F to 80°F should be fine for both of you. Check the manual that comes with your machine for its recommended temperature range. The relative humidity should be between 20 and 80 percent. By the way, store floppys between 50° and 125°F.

Setting Up Your Printer

Printers are attached by either an RS232 serial connector or a parallel connector. As mentioned earlier, the parallel connecter sends the printer *characters* one at a time, while the serial type sends *bits* one at a time. Lower cost printers always use parallel; higher cost ones always use serial. The major difference between them is the distance over which they can be used. Parallel connections are good for about 8-10 feet. The serial is rated for 50 feet, but I've heard of them used to cable printers as far away as two hundred feet from the word processor. The serial connector has 25 pins on the connector. Most printers require only three to six wires in the cable. Don't waste your money on a cable with 25 wires. Check the specs on your computer and printer before purchasing the cable. Or better yet, purchase the correct cable with the printer.

I advise locating the printer on a surface separate from the word processor because the vibrations and noise can be quite annoying. Place the printer on a stable surface to ensure that mechanical vibrations will not cause your printer to fall off. Position the printer so you can easily get at and change both the ribbon and paper. Most commercial printer tables have slots in them for feeding the paper from a box placed underneath. I constructed a little shelf for my printer with the paper stored below. The paper does jam at times, so leave yourself sufficient space to get behind the printer to re-thread the paper. Most printers use tractor feed, requiring paper with removable strips with punched holes on the sides. You can purchase a 3000 sheet box of paper for about $30. Some outfits will supply paper with your letterhead printed on it for a bit more. A single sheet feeder may be purchased for most printers that can also feed envelopes. The one drawback is that the single sheet feeder may cost as much as the printer.

If you have a daisy wheel printer, save the plastic cases the daisy wheels come in or get a case that will hold several wheels. The wheels are fragile and you don't want to break off any petals. There are also daisy wheel cleaning kits which come with a holder and cleaner solution for about $10. These can make an arduous task rather easy.

A vacuum cleaner with a thin nozzle is great for occasionally cleaning out paper dust that accumulates in the printer. Also, keep spare ribbons around. I purchased a new model matrix printer for my word processor, only to find that there would not be any spare ribbons available for at least a couple of months. The print was getting quite faint when a friend told me that squirting WD-40 (a standard automotive and hardware lubricant) on a worn ribbon rejuvenates it. With no chance of getting a new ribbon, I tried it. To my amazement it worked, making my ribbon as good as new. If you try this and something weird happens to your printer, please don't come after me. All I'm saying is it worked fine on my printer. But if you try it, you're on your own.

There are also very inexpensive ribbon inkers that will rejuvenate a ribbon by putting a fresh supply of ink on it. A friend once used one of these to re-ink one of my WD-40'd ribbons. When I got it back I couldn't tell the difference between it and a brand new one.

Disk Drives

Disk drives require a relatively dust-free and jostle-free environment. With normal use the read/write heads of a disk drive build up an oxide coating which should be cleaned off every few months. A floppy disk cleaning kit (a floppy disk with a cloth disk in the center and a bottle of solvent) may be purchased for about $25. Just squirt the magic chemical (which is mainly alcohol) on the cloth and insert the disk into the drive as if it were a normal floppy. Issuing the load program or read file command tricks the disk drive into attempting to read the disk, at which point the read/write head gets a bath. I have not seen any cleaning kits for the Winchester drives, but there are cleaning kits for the removable cartridge hard disks.

Floppy Disks

As I mentioned in Chapter 5, the main factors that shorten a floppy disk's life are spindle hole deformation and improper handling. There is a spindle hole insert which supposedly prolongs the life of a disk, but I've never purchased one. Instead, I always buy high quality disks rather than cheapies. A high quality disk spins quietly in the drive. Stick with brand names.

You don't clean floppys. The jacket has a lint-free liner that cleans the disk every time it spins. If it gets dirty from fingerprints or someone spilling Gatorade on it, just throw it out. I've found floppy disks to be quite reliable. In seven years of working with microcomputers I've had only four or five disks fail. That's not bad, and keeping backup disks made those times easy to deal with.

For storing disks, there are a variety of cases that open up, fold out and even have magnetic-proof shielded pages. I prefer going down to the local supermarket and buying a recipe case for $5 rather than paying $35 for a similar case from a computer store.

On occasion I have used single density disks on my double density drives. (Since I'm a cheapskate, I wasn't about to throw away those perfectly good old disks I had lying around.) Does it work? Yes, except on some disks an error occurs when formatting the innermost tracks. I use my disk lock-out program which defines a file to exist over the bad region. I lose a couple of K of storage, but I'm using those oldies but goodies. I advise buying double density disks unless you come upon single density disks that are just too good a deal to pass up.

Another trick I use to reduce my disk cost is to punch several holes in the disk jacket to enable my machine to read and write information to both sides of the disk (see illustration). Once the holes are punched, you can flip the disk over and use the other side.

The only problem with using the flip side of the disk is that the lint-free liner that cleans the disk rotates in only one direction. If you flip the disk over, it now rotates in the opposite direction. The disk experts claim that all the dirt picked up in the liner is now wiped back onto the surface. Well, they are probably right. So what I do is use the reverse side for occasional use only. I do things

HOW TO MAKE A FLIPPABLE FLOPPY

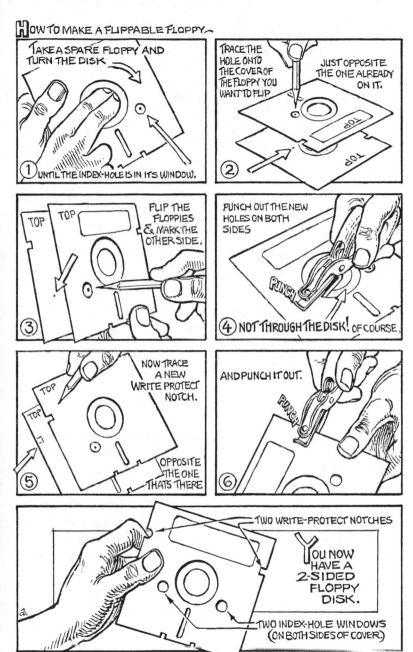

① TAKE A SPARE FLOPPY AND TURN THE DISK UNTIL THE INDEX-HOLE IS IN ITS WINDOW.

② TRACE THE HOLE ONTO THE COVER OF THE FLOPPY YOU WANT TO FLIP JUST OPPOSITE THE ONE ALREADY ON IT.

③ FLIP THE FLOPPIES & MARK THE OTHER SIDE.

④ PUNCH OUT THE NEW HOLES ON BOTH SIDES. PUNCH. NOT THROUGH THE DISK! OF COURSE.

⑤ NOW TRACE A NEW WRITE PROTECT NOTCH. OPPOSITE THE ONE THATS THERE.

⑥ AND PUNCH IT OUT. PUNCH.

TWO WRITE-PROTECT NOTCHES

YOU NOW HAVE A 2-SIDED FLOPPY DISK.

TWO INDEX-HOLE WINDOWS (ON BOTH SIDES OF COVER.)

like backing up disks on the backside of floppys (backside backup).
Try it. The money you save will more than pay you back for this book.

The Log Book

If more than one person will be using a machine, it's a good idea
to attach a log book to it. This book should contain all the standard
operating procedures, a summary of command instructions, and a
list of critical phone numbers including the repair and service
number. Most important are recovery procedures—what to do
when the machine stops working.

The log book also should have a section for users to write down
any problems that occurred while they used the machine. This is a
great way to keep track of sporadic problems.

Trouble Shooting
(or, What Do I Do When It Doesn't?)

Problem: *You turn on the power switch and the screen comes up
blank, or you are working on the machine and the screen goes blank.*
A blank screen means the system is not getting power. Check to
see if the power plug has slipped out of the outlet. If the plug is
firmly in the outlet, see if there is power from the outlet itself by
plugging something else, such as a desk lamp, into the outlet. If the
lamp goes on, there's power; if it doesn't, check the fuse box or
circuit breaker for the outlet.

If the power's OK, check the *machine's* circuit breaker. This is
usually a small button located on the back of the machine. Press it
in and release it. If the machine goes back on you're ready to start
working again. Circuit breakers are designed to protect a computer's circuitry. Sometimes they switch off on their own, but usually
there's a good reason. So be alert; if the circuit breaker clicks out
again, either the system has overheated or there's a power supply
problem. Turn off the machine for awhile and try it again later. If it
works, try lowering the room temperature. If it still doesn't work
contact your local service person.

Problem: *The machine stops dead with information displayed on the screen. Pressing keys on the keyboard has no effect.*
Try pressing the ESCAPE key. This may start the machine operating again. If a print command had just been entered and the printer was not turned on (or is out of paper) the system will freeze. If this is your problem read ahead to printer problems.

This condition also occurs when the connector cable from the keyboard to the computer has come loose. If none of these is your problem, try turning the machine off and then on again. The freeze could have been caused by an electrical disturbance. Note it in the log book. If it happens a lot, it might indicate the need for line conditioning or an anti-static mat.

Problem: *The text storage disk drive attempts to read continuously. The drive light stays on and a whirring sound comes from the drive.*
This will happen if you forgot to put a disk in the drive and the word processor is attempting to read or write on that drive. Press the reset button to cancel the disk command. If that does not work, turn off the system and restart it. Now, on some systems you can insert a disk while the drive is on, but this is a risky procedure. So test it on an expendable disk before trying it on an important disk.

Problem: *The disk drive does not respond to disk commands, but the keyboard is operational.*
If the drives are separate from the computer, check the connecting cables and power cables to the drives.

Problem: *An attempt to read from a disk results in garbled characters on the screen or a disk error message.*
This happens when the operating system cannot read the information from a disk file. There could have been a power line problem as the file was being written. Extraneous information can be written on a disk left in a disk drive while the system power is turned on or off. A magnet placed close to the disk or excessive dirt can also cause disk reading problems. If you have a backup disk you can smile—take it out and just continue working.

If you don't have a backup, use your *system disk utility verification program* to find out where the problem is. The verification program will locate and lock out the problem areas of the disk and you can then copy the remainder of the disk by using the copy or backup program. If your system does not come with a verification program, you can purchase one for around $50. I got mine free from my local user group—another good reason to join.

If you continue to have disk problems, go back and read the section on the care and handling of diskettes in Chapter 5. If you are handling the disks carefully, start looking for magnets, or have someone check your power lines. I once purchased and returned a box of disks that had seven faulty disks in the box. Fortunately, this occurrence is relatively rare. Bad disks will usually be discovered when you attempt to format them.

Problem: *You start the system and the screen fills with nonsense characters and the drive may run continuously.*

You have placed a text file disk into the system drive. The machine is looking for the operating system and can't find it. Remove disks from the drives, turn the power off and restart the system using the systems disk.

Problem: *One of the disk drives stops working and it's not a cable connection problem.*

This once happened to me; I continued working on the system using only one drive until I could get an appointment with the repair shop. Using my backup systems disk, I erased all the parts of the word processor program I did not need, like the menu display screens. This gave me more space on the systems disk to store my text. When my other drive was repaired, I copied my text from the systems disk and replaced the parts of the program I had removed. This technique can be made to work with either the systems or text drive.

Problem: *The printer stops working.*

Look for disconnected cables or small pieces of jammed paper. The cover may not be on properly, or the printer may be out of paper. Check the printer indicator lights which indicate the status of the printer. If you have to take your printer to the repair shop, short term rental of another could keep your system running while the repair is being made. A call for help to your system user group might turn up someone who will let you print on her or his system.

Service

Any other problems will require a service call. Here's where belonging to a user group comes in handy. The place you bought your machine may not be the best place for repairs. Call the user group to see if any of its members had a similar problem. If someone has, they could help you get a handle on what your problem is and what it will cost to fix it. Find out which dealers are the best for repairs or if there are local independents who really know their stuff. If you have a service contract, or the machine is still under warranty, call and get it back to the dealer immediately.

Compared to my cars, the small computers I've owned have been incredibly reliable. They have provided literally thousands of hours of trouble-free service. I may be sorry someday, but I have never had a maintenance contract on any of my machines. I have had only two minor repair problems—that's pretty good for seven years. If you want advice on whether to buy a maintenance contract for your machine, talk to some other users. They'll be able to tell you about the problems they've had on their machines.

And last but not least remember Stern's Golden Rule—"When all else fails, read the instruction manual."

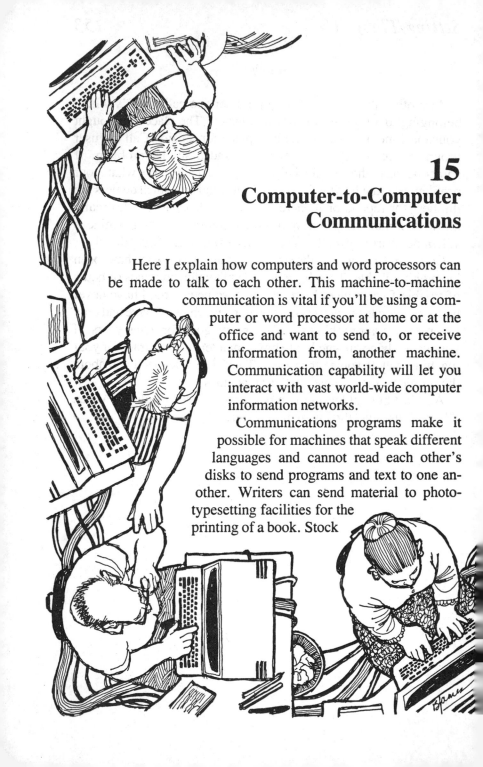

15
Computer-to-Computer Communications

Here I explain how computers and word processors can be made to talk to each other. This machine-to-machine communication is vital if you'll be using a computer or word processor at home or at the office and want to send to, or receive information from, another machine. Communication capability will let you interact with vast world-wide computer information networks.

Communications programs make it possible for machines that speak different languages and cannot read each other's disks to send programs and text to one another. Writers can send material to photo-typesetting facilities for the printing of a book. Stock market afficionados can get the latest Dow Jones reports, and lovers can send messages across the miles.

How Computer Communications Works

Let's start out with a definition: *computer communications* refers to the transfer of information from one computer or word processor to another. If you're travelling around a city you might take a bus. Information in a computer does the same. It travels around on what's called an electrical *bus*. A computer bus doesn't have wheels; it's a group of wires or electrical connections that move electronic information from one place to another. If you're travelling between two cities, you might go to a station or a port, board a vehicle, and be taken to a port or station at your destination. Likewise, information leaving a word processor moves on the computer bus to the *input/output* (I/O) *port* where it's then sent over wires to the port of a destination machine. Computer ports are, therefore, where information leaves or enters the machine. Travel destinations can be to another computer, a printer, the disk drives, or some other place you might care to send information.

Travel plans? Information is either transported in serial form from a serial port or in parallel form from a parallel port.

The serial port transfers or receives information one bit at a time on a single wire. This means that the eight information bits representing each character are sent over the *output* or "send" line of the serial port as a kind of telegraph transmission of dots and dashes. The serial port is designed to send information between two machines that are up to 50 feet apart, but serial transfer at distances of a couple of hundred feet are commonplace.

Parallel ports, on the other hand, send or receive information in the form of individual characters or bytes. Because a byte is eight bits, eight wires—each carrying 1 bit of information—are required for parallel transfer. So the parallel port is like having eight telegraph lines working simultaneously to send out information. Faster? It sure is—at least eight times faster. And that's why disk drives almost always send and receive data through parallel I/O ports. But there is one major problem with parallel travel, it has to be used for distances less than around 12 feet because it's difficult to keep the signals on all the wires synchronized (marching at the same pace). So if your information is going farther than across the room it has to go serial.

Setting Up the Communications Connection

The most common direct computer-to-computer connection is made by wiring the two machines together the same way a serial printer is wired to a word processor. As a matter of fact, a serial RS232 connection is one way to get a word processor to communicate with a printer. This same RS232 connection can be used to cable two word processors together. If you plan to have a system with a serial printer and communications capability, make sure it comes with two separate RS232 ports—one for the printer and one for communications.

If you are connecting machines that are more than a couple of hundred feet apart, there is a device called a *line driver* that boosts the signal and extends the maximum distance for serial transfer to as much as a mile. Instead of wiring the machines directly to each other, each machine is cabled to a separate line driver, and the two line drivers are wired together.

Modems

What if you can't wire the machines directly? An indirect connection can be made using the telephone, plus a *modem*. A modem is a computer's "telephone." It attaches to the same serial port, but instead of sending dots and dashes on a wire, it sends and receives the dots and dashes as audible tones on the telephone line. Like telephones, modems come in a variety of sizes and shapes, each with its own specialized functions. A modem will let your word processor send or receive information anywhere phone lines go. (As a matter of fact there are nearly as many computers talking on the phone lines as people.) Of course, both the sending and receiving computers need modems and RS232 connections.

Modems come in two basic types, the *acoustic coupler* and the *direct connect,* and cost $75-$600.

The acoustic coupler communicates through the handset (the part you talk into) of a standard telephone. It has two rubber cups to accommodate the handset into which it beeps tones corresponding to the dots and dashes (bits of information) being sent.

The direct connect modem bips and beeps as well, but rather than using a phone handset, it plugs into a phone jack. The only reason to get the acoustic coupler rather than the direct connect modem is to transfer data from offices, hotels or phone booths, where there isn't an accessible phone jack. A battery-operated acoustic coupler can be used on any phone anywhere.

There are three modem classifications: *originate, answer* and *originate/answer devices.* If you are using your computer and modem to call another computer at a business office, a *phototypesetter,* an information utility, or your honey's house, and won't be receiving calls from any of these places—you can use an *originate-only* modem. The business office, phototypesetter, information utility, and honey need *answer-mode* modems. Those of you who sometimes call and sometimes answer calls from computers and word processors need an *originate/answer* modem. These have a switch that lets you use them in either mode. On the other hand, if you know you'll only be initiating calls, you can save about 25 percent by purchasing an originate-only modem.

Modems can work in what is called *full duplex* or *half duplex* modes. Full duplex allows both machines to talk and listen at the same time and works like a telephone. Half duplex lets only one machine talk at a time, like a CB radio. Most small computers use full duplex mode for sending information between machines. With full duplex, if you are keyboarding information to a remote machine you are assured that every key you press is received correctly. The communications link sends each character out the port through the modem over the phone line into the receiving modem and computer. As each character is received, it is sent back across the line and displayed on your machine's screen. What you see is what they got. It's an acknowledgement of the receipt of your transmission. This technique is also called *echoplexing* and requires one end to be a terminal and the other a "host" that echoes the characters back. A full duplex mode also could be set up for two machines to send things to each other simultaneously. Unlike people, computers can talk and listen at the same time without missing a word.

The last of the modem options are *direct dial* and *auto answer*. The direct dial option lets your word processor dial another machine automatically when you tell it to do so. The auto answer modem enables your word processor to answer the phone when another computer calls. The direct dial and auto answer options add about $200 to the basic modem price. Sounds like science fiction doesn't it? Do you think they call each other when they get lonely?

Bits and Bytes of Communications

There is still another way to classify modems and that is by the transmission speed or the number of bits that can be sent in a second. The most common modems for use with dial-up phones send and receive information at either 300 or 1200 bits per second (bps or bits/sec), sometimes erroneously called "baud." Now, be careful in your calculations since *asynchronous communications,* the least costly and most common means for data transfer, sends a single character at a time. In order to alert the modem and the second computer that a character is coming down the line, a "start" bit is sent before the character and a "stop" bit is sent after it. This means that each character transmitted is represented by ten bits instead of the standard eight bits. To determine the character transfer rate of a modem (characters per second), divide the bit rate by ten not eight. So a 300 bps modem transfers 300/10, or 30 characters per second. A 300 bps modem costs $60 to $200; a 1200 bps modem costs $300 to $600.

Now that you know all the mathematics and have the cost data, which speed do you choose? Well, to transfer the 1500 characters of text that are on a standard double spaced page takes 50 seconds with a 300 bps modem (1500/30), but only 13 seconds with a 1200 bps modem (1500/120). So if you're transferring a 200-page manuscript, it will take 2 hours and 46 minutes with the 300 bps modem,compared to a little over 40 minutes with the faster unit. So, Peter Piper, which is the better buy? You'll have to weigh your phone time charges and the amount of time your machine is tied up in communications against the higher purchase price of a faster modem. Be aware that local phone companies that do not currently bill for the time on a local call will be doing so in the near future. As the days of long and relatively free, local computer-to-computer communications draws to an end, we will be seeing a lot more 1200 bps modems in use.

If you decide to purchase a 1200 bps modem, make sure it will also work at 300 bps. You never know when someone with a slower modem might decide to call. To ensure that modems beep a compatible language there are a set of standards for devices sold by Bell Telephone. A 300 bps modem should be 103/113 compatible and 1200 bps modems should be what is called 212/103 compatible. It's like making sure you speak the language of the country you're in. You can get by speaking a different language, but you'll have a lot fewer people to talk with. A final bits and bytes point is that when machines can be wired to each other the bit rate restriction of the modem no longer applies. I usually run direct wire connect communication at 9600 bps and sometimes, if I am lucky, at 19,200 bps. Saves a lot of time when the machines are talking in person—er, machine—Oh never mind, you know what I mean.

Communications Software

As always, for a computer or word processor to do anything it requires software. A communication program enables two computers to talk with each other, by direct wiring or over the phone lines with modems. Somewhat similar to strangers meeting at a party, computers must be properly introduced, speak the same language, and observe the same rules of etiquette or protocol if they're to have meaningful communications. The communication software plays the role of a skillful host, encoding and translating the electronic signals in just the right manner for the two computers to accept and make sense of each other's transmission.

On many systems, a communications program is supplied as a standard part of the operating system or the word processor software. If you're not satisfied with the communications program supplied with your system, or if none came with it, a lot of commercial programs are available in the $50 to $200 range. These programs come in three levels of sophistication.

The first level will set your machine up to function as what's known as a *dumb terminal,* that is, a machine capable of transmitting only what you type on the keyboard and displaying received material on the video screen. This is fine if you're calling your office to check on the mail in your electronic mailbox or if you're calling a local information utility to get current stock prices. These programs will let you print out information as it is received. The major problem in working with a dumb terminal is you might be referred to as a dumb terminal user.

The next level of communication programs enables you to capture a transmission on a floppy disk file for later viewing. This means you don't have to take the time to read or print the material as it is received. You can read it from the text storage disk after hanging up the phone. This can be important if you are paying for each minute of telephone time, or even worse, paying for computer time on the other end of the connection.

The most sophisticated communications program can send a series of documents or even programs, in what is called, *batch mode,* from one system's disk files to another's. The better packages compress the transmitted information to reduce the transmission time and phone line expense. In this technique, the communications program analyzes the text to be transmitted and encodes it to reduce the number of bytes required. The program in the receiving machine then decompresses or decodes the text to its original form. Typical size reduction on text files is around 50 percent. How do they do it? Magic!

Some communication programs will also provide character block error checking procedures, or *cyclic redundancy checking.* This is a way for the communicating machines to check if phone line "noise" changed the content of any of the transmitted information. If the receiving machine detects an error, its program automatically requests the sending program to re-transmit the portions in error. It is all done automatically by the programs. I would never send program or data files over the phone lines without error-checking software. A couple of phone line blips could play havoc with a large part of a transmission. It's not as critical with text files because these are in readable English and errors can easily be spotted and corrected. If your local phone lines are notorious for background blips and bleeps, or if the stuff you're sending is really important, make sure your communications program has block error checking in it.

Communications software is also available to let small computers or word processors speak the same language spoken by large mainframe computer networks. Most large businesses are beginning to realize that a small computer with word processing capability or a stand alone word processor may cost less than a terminal for a mainframe computer. So, they are buying these instead of expensive terminals that can only be terminals.

If you will be sending files of information back and forth to a mainframe computer, you'll require a communications program that sends files in block form in what is called *synchronous transmission* mode. These programs send data as blocks of characters without the start and stop bits you find in asynchronous transmissions. I will not go into these in detail, but if you need to send very large document files at rapid transmission speeds (4800-9600 bps), synchronous systems could be vital. Synchronous transmission requires a synchronous modem and a specialized synchronous serial port.

Automatic Communications

Let's say you are using your machine at home rather than going to an office. One day while you're out on important business your boss decides it's urgent that you see a copy of a report or proposal. She wants to send the report to your machine even though you're not there. Sounds complex? Well, it's not. But you do need some special things to make it possible.

First, the modem on your system has to be the more expensive kind with an *auto answer* function. You also need a "comm program" that can respond when the modem answers the phone, and then receive information and store it on a disk file. So before leaving your home, turn on your machine, load in the communication program and enter the parameters that tell it to receive a file. The program then starts examining the input serial port. But nothing is there . . . yet. You told it to receive information, so it just sits there and patiently waits. More faithful than your dog Bonzo, it'll wait forever if it must. Then your boss calls, using her modem in *originate* mode. The phone rings, your modem answers and sends a signal to the RS232 port to tell your machine to do its thing. Your comm program then sends a message like "Hi there, what file do you want to send?"

The message appears on your boss' machine. She then enters the names of the files she'll be sending; your comm program then sends a message to go ahead. She instructs her comm program to send the files. From here on the machines do their own thing, sending, receiving and re-transmitting messages until the communication is complete. Then your communications program tells your modem to hang up the phone and goes back to watching the input port for another call. It's like a fancy answering machine. If your friends complain when they call and get your answering machine, imagine what they'll say when they call and get your computer beeping at them. By the way, usually an auto answer modem will hang up the phone if there is no computer beep from the other end within seven seconds.

Here's another example of automatic transmittal. Suppose I decide to send my publisher the last three chapters of this book as soon as they are finished (he's been hounding me for months). The phone call is from Chevy Chase, Maryland to Santa Fe, New Mexico. Rather than pay high cost daytime phone rates, I set up the machine to run the comm program in auto dial mode. The program asks what time to dial and the names of the files to be transferred. I enter 11:05 pm and the file names for Chapters 14, 15 and 16. At 11:05 my word processor dials the JMP office and gets a busy signal. Peter, who always works late, is on the phone. My machine hangs up and redials. It keeps dialing until Peter gets off the phone. The phone rings, JMP's machine answers it and asks my machine if there is anything to send. My machine starts sending the chapters, and when it's finished, it says goodbye. In the morning, Ken checks the JMP machine and there are the overdue chapters.

Do you get the gist? There are a lot of ways to use modems and communications programs. Buy what you need for the jobs you do. And don't feel bad if no one calls your machine when you're not around. Unlike humans, machines can get along for years without communicating with anyone. My machine never gets calls and it's in good spirits.

Electronic Mail

The previous descriptions were examples of word processors sending and receiving information. This process of electronic interchange is normally referred to as *electronic mail*. To establish the electronic mail process on a larger scale requires a machine devoted to receiving and sending information. This is sometimes referred to as a bulletin board system. The computer runs a large scale communications program that answers phone calls, relays messages, updates files and delivers mail—kind of like an electronic postman. Once you have a comm program that lets your word processor receive messages or files through an auto answer modem, you have the beginnings of an electronic mail system. Many offices are now using a small computer system and modem for this purpose. Anyone who knows the computer code can call the machine to leave or fetch messages.

Speaking of bulletin board programs, there are bulletin board programs (in the public domain) available for free through most local user groups. Currently, there are over a thousand public service bulletin boards using these programs and answering phones around the country. Once you sign on to one of these systems, you'll find provisions to let you "down load" or copy any programs that you might want (including the bulletin board program), leave messages, or donate your own programs. The people operating the bulletin boards are people like you and me who have decided to attach their computer to a telephone when they're not using it.

The hero of this revolution is Ward Christianson, who wrote the first bulletin board program and placed it in the public domain rather than selling it for thousands of dollars. It is refreshing to realize that Christianson and the people running bulletin boards actually exist. I have included a nationwide listing of bulletin board phone numbers as Appendix IV. Call them and join the revolution. Use the message facility to get answers to problems when they occur. Feel free to take copies of programs and, even more important, make sure to donate your own programs!

Many companies now operate bulletin board systems enabling employees or clients to send files and make inquiries any time of the day or night. These systems usually have security measures to make sure only authorized people (computers, actually) are using the system. This kind of electronic mail system requires a communication program and one modem for each phone line it will be answering. The system can also accept messages from terminals directly wired into one of its ports. A multi-user electronic mail system can talk to and receive messages from many systems simultaneously.

Electronic Mail Networks—The Information Utilities

Several major computer companies have established nationwide networks of communicating computers. One of the services offered by these companies is a nationwide electronic mail service. This means that as a subscriber I can make a local call to get on the network and send anything to any other subscriber in the country. The other subscriber then would make a local phone call to the computer and fetch the information.

Although you save on long distance phone bills, you must pay a network subscription fee plus an hourly network use fee, which ranges from $5 to $17 depending on the time of day. Both sender and receiver are billed a minimum of $5 per hour, whether they're across the street from each other or across the nation. It's quite a bit different from phone service where rates are dependent on distance. It's a real bargain for transfer of important documents requiring immediate delivery. Another advantage of the *information utility* approach over phone company service is what is called "store and forward message service," which means that the message is sent and if the receiving party is not there, it'll wait for her. Another benefit: you can send the same information to a whole lot of people in one shot.

A disadvantage of the information utility approach is that, even if there is no mail in your electronic box, you have to pay to find out. Also, right now there is no way to send or receive pictures with any of the electronic mail systems. Imagine what this book would look like without Peter's and Betsy's illustrations. However, there are facsimile transmission machines and facsimile networks for transmitting pictures. These have very little to do with word processors. They're relatives of the photocopier, working the way Xerox machines would if they could be made to talk on telephones.

What else do these utilities offer that might be worth $5 per hour? The most well known of the utilities are *The Source,* owned by Readers Digest, and *Compuserve,* owned by H & R Block. Each claims to have about 25,000 subscribers. In addition to electronic mail, they offer services such as access to the nationwide airline reservation system, a bulletin board system resembling electronic classified ads, a library of computer programs and access for running them on their mainframe, and a CB type communications ability that allows anyone logged on the system to rap with whoever else is on the system wanting to play CB. 10-4 Good Buddy.

And there is even electronic publishing. For a moderate fee you can store a book, article or computer program in an electronic library accessible to any of the subscribers. You then receive a royalty based on the amount of time subscribers spend looking at, playing with or using your material. Publishing companies beware!

For the business-minded there are services that offer minute-to-minute stock prices, as well as electronic banking. For those of you with infomaniac tendencies, the names and addresses of some of the more popular utilities are listed in Appendix III.

An autodial modem and comm program can be set up to access the information utilities service after hours when the rates are lower. You can capture the material at transmission speeds and store it on your text storage disk. Then you can read it leisurely with breakfast coffee without worrying about the meter running while you read.

Phototypesetting

Phototypesetting is the primary means of book preparation for printing. The process uses a fancy word processor to create text in photographic form. You can think of the phototypesetter or photo-compositor as a machine that creates and takes pictures of high quality, electronically generated pages of print. These photographic prints are used to make the printing plates used on a printing press.

A phototypesetter is a specialized word processor with a fancy display screen that measures the characters on a line in a character width fraction, or picas, and prints the text photographically. Before the era of low-cost word processors, all printed material was keyboarded by operators. Therefore, you paid a fee for the operator's time and the typesetting equipment.

Communicating word processors now make it possible to transmit material directly from disk storage files to the phototypesetting machine by a phone call. This not only eliminates the keyboarding fee, but also eliminates the need for proofreading the second keyboarding. To do this, you need a modem, a comm program and a conversion table that correlates the symbols used by your word processor with the symbols used by the typesetting machine. The table is sent from your machine to the typesetter as the first piece of text. Most typesetters with communication capability contain tables for the more popular word processing systems. Special functions can be entered into the standard tables. After the text is received by the typesetter, all that's needed is formatting for the proportional spacing and layout.

The cost of the job is reduced by about 25 percent from the normal cost when an operator is used. Many local typesetters have installed auto answer modems so that text can be sent at any time.

If you have a word processor program that will drive a printer capable of proportional printing (remember, each space allocated to the character is a function of the character's size), you may be able to bypass the phototypesetting process. First, you need a precision daisy wheel proportional printer, or a high quality precision matrix printer with a single-strike high quality carbon ribbon. Print the material on the best quality paper, leaving space for illustrations and pictures. The printed output can be brought to the print shop and used for creating the printing plates. If you are thinking about using this process, make sure you talk with the person who does the printing first.

Communication Between Incompatible Machines

What do you do if you want to send text files between two word processors that use completely different text file formats, which is true of most word processors? There are a limited number of costly programs that convert formats and if you can find one that works for the two systems which are trying to communicate, then you're all set. However, there is a simple solution that is worth its weight in gold. All word processor programs let you store files on disk in print format (see Chapter 5). This means that the text is stored as a stream of characters that contain margins, spaces, headings, and carriage returns exactly as if you had typed them in. These files are called *teletype* or *TTY* files. Now, here's the good news: TTY files can easily be printed on any system. So, if you want to send the files and have them printed at another location, TTY will do the job. They don't tell you this, but most word processors will let you edit files in TTY format. At worst, you might have to do a global change to get rid of the carriage returns and margin spacing, but it can be done with little hassle.

One final point. In order to create a TTY file your word processor must be set to print to a teletype terminal. If it's set to print to a precision printer, the file will contain a lot of extraneous characters that make no sense at all.

Telecommuting and the Electronic Cottage Industry

Within this decade we may well see the decline of the American office. Increasing numbers of people in a variety of businesses are *telecommuting;* that is, working at home with small computers and word processors linked electronically to central business offices. I've already explained how to set up the telephone linkage. So all that is required is convincing your employer that it will cost less to have you work at home. Many organizations are setting up programs for employees to work at home on a part or full-time basis. Unions are concerned that payment by piecework will turn the Electronic Cottages into Electronic Sweatshops. So, if you'll be setting up this type of arrangement, remind your employer that he'll be saving on a desk, office space and phone installation. You, in turn, will be eligible for tax benefits for the portior of your living space allotted for work functions, as well as saving on commuting, meals and other work-away-from-home expenses. Weigh all of these factors carefully in negotiating your working arrangements.

For working parents, at first the Electronic Cottage appears to be a blessing. My experience has been a limited blessing. Heather was born at about the time I began writing the first draft of this book. Betsy (my wife, not the illustrator) went back to work when Heather was three months old. I decided I would take care of Heather and write the book. That lasted about a month before I realized that I could not handle both roles. We made day-care arrangements and Heather now hangs out with a great family about three days a week. I mention this only to inform you of the difficulty I found in keeping my work separate from my home and family responsibilities. Think about being in constant close proximity to the refrigerator, the dog, people dropping in to visit, and the thousand and one other intrusions you'll have to learn to live with if your cottage industry is going to survive.

Telecommuting does not require a full scale word processor and printer. You can use a low cost *telecomputer*, which has keyboard, modem and small display screen. It has limited memory and no external storage, but it will work for keyboard input to an office computer. Many salespeople are starting to carry these around with them. They're available for $200-700. They keep getting smaller and smaller. The next step is a wrist watch that plays Pac Man, tells the time and lets you phone your computer. Science fiction? Nope— no more than some things you'll find in computer stores right now.

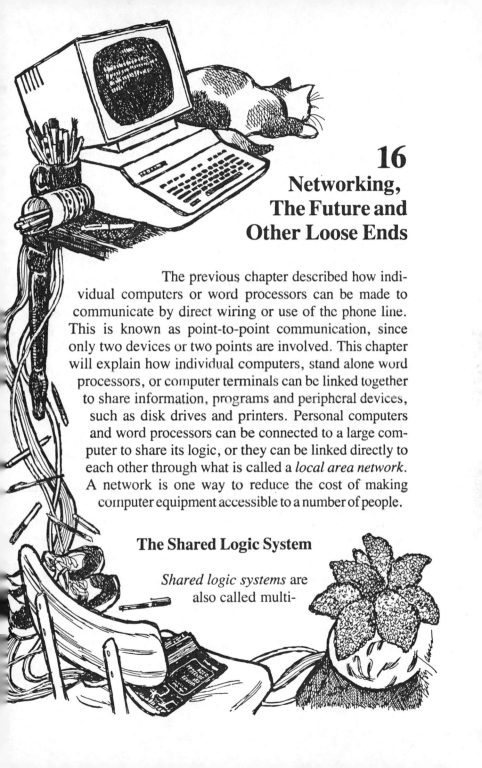

16
Networking, The Future and Other Loose Ends

The previous chapter described how individual computers or word processors can be made to communicate by direct wiring or use of the phone line. This is known as point-to-point communication, since only two devices or two points are involved. This chapter will explain how individual computers, stand alone word processors, or computer terminals can be linked together to share information, programs and peripheral devices, such as disk drives and printers. Personal computers and word processors can be connected to a large computer to share its logic, or they can be linked directly to each other through what is called a *local area network*. A network is one way to reduce the cost of making computer equipment accessible to a number of people.

The Shared Logic System

Shared logic systems are also called multi-user or time-sharing systems because they let more than one person use the same computer at the same time. The early shared logic systems were very large, expensive machines capable of performing tasks for hundreds of users at a time. These very powerful machines are still used by large companies, and are the network controllers for the major information utilities such as *The Source* and *Compuserve.*

Now the new generation of small computers we use for processing words and as general purpose tools are also capable of working with more than one person at a time. The difference between a computer that works with only one person at a time and one that works with lots of people is—you guessed it—software!

Shared logic systems require a fancy operating system which divides the machine's memory into sections for each user's program. The operating system also divides the computer's processing time so everyone gets a share. As you'd probably guess, the more people using the system, the slower it runs. Those of us who are used to an instant response when a key is pressed might become quite annoyed when things start to slow down because lots of people are on the system.

Even the smallest of the word processing computers, the 8-bit machines, can become multi-user systems. CP/M, the standard 8-bit operating system, has a big brother called MP/M, a multi-user operating system. Purchase a copy of MP/M, install it on your machine, attach some additional terminals to the auxiliary serial ports, and several people can start processing.

"Wait a minute!" you say. "My machine only has two serial ports and I'm using them for a printer and a modem." Well, you'll either have to upgrade your machine to add some more ports or, if that's not possible, get another machine. However, I don't recommend using an 8-bit machine if there will be more than two or three people using the system. Eight bitters just don't have the speed and capacity to handle lots of people doing word processing. Companies selling 8-bit multi-user machines claim that as many as eight people can simultaneously work on the machine. I think what they're really saying is that two or three people can work while five or six people hang around and kibbitz.

For a truly versatile, multi-user system you should consider a 16- or 32-bit machine running under an operating system such as Unix. The machine should have a large available memory of from 250K to 1 megabyte. Each user will require a separate video display terminal and RS232 cabling to the system. If you want to attach a stand alone word processor or a personal computer to a multi-user system, it must contain a communications program that at minimum makes it appear like a dumb terminal. One or more of the available serial ports can easily accommodate modems, allowing users to call and access the system from remote locations. Be aware that communication speeds available over a phone line are extremely slow and, as such, are unsuitable for effective word processing. But the modem connections will work well for transferring and receiving files from remote locations and for electronic mail functions.

Some disadvantages of a multi-user system are:

a) If the central computer stops working, everyone stops working.
b) The response time of the system is dependent on how many people are using the system.
c) All communications between individual users must go through the central computer.

Networking

In contrast to shared logic systems, a *network* is a means of linking computers, printers, disk drives and other peripheral devices together without going through a central computer. In the best of all possible worlds, the network serves as a bridge between what might be incompatible computers and word processors. The advantage of a network, in contrast to a time sharing or multiprocessing system, is that the system's performance does not decrease as more people use it. Also, if one computer breaks down the network does not stop functioning, since all of the individual machines can still work on their own.

The idea behind networking is the sharing of the expensive system parts, such as the printer and hard disk. A single printer could be used by any of the individuals on the network, and one large scale hard disk could easily handle the text storage needs of the entire network. Of course, each individual user can still have their own floppy disk drives and draft quality printer. In short, there are lots of ways to configure a network.

There are a number of networks on the market that allow individuals to have their own dedicated word processors while sharing large capacity disks and expensive printers. These systems require a separate central computer to handle the requests from the networked machines to read and write information on a disk or to print on a central printer. This type of network, often called a *shared resource system,* is a simple way to set up communal access to storage files. In contrast to the multi-user system, the users on a shared resource system each have a stand alone machine capable of working without the network. However, if the control computer (or *disk server*, as it is called) breaks down, the files on the central disk become inaccessible.

Local Area Networks

A local area network is a communication network connecting lots of different machines, separated by less than several thousand feet. Thus the name, *local area network.* These nets can be configured as a *bus network* in which each of the individual computers is attached to a common cable or bus, or as a *ring network* in which the machines are linked to each other to form a ring.

The operation of the bus network is similar to an intercom where all of the individual phones are attached by a tap box to a central cable or bus. This means when someone talks on the network, everyone else can hear what he says. It's like using a sophisticated CB radio with everyone wired to a central cable. I say sophisticated because the local area network tap box, or *control interface unit,* that connects computers to the network will only receive information addressed to it. It can hear everything going on but only accepts information addressed to it.

The control interface unit either attaches to the computer's port or is plugged in internally. The control unit automatically handles the sending and receiving of network information in a way that's totally unnoticeable to you. It can detect errors in received messages and request that they be retransmitted. Control of the network is decentralized so anyone who has a message to send to anyone else controls the network while the message is being sent.

Because there is no central controller, each control unit must be able to recognize when two or more machines are starting to send information at the same time, since this would result in jumbled information going onto the network. When this type of transmission collision occurs, all the devices involved stop transmitting and do the equivalent of an electronic coin flip to see who gets to send their information. This resolution of simultaneous transmission is called *collision detection*. Under normal operations the process of determining who gets to transmit is called a *protocol*. In computerese it's called a *contention protocol with collision detection;* we call it service on a first come, first served basis.

Information in the ring network is handled by a relay passing technique. Each machine on the network receives the message and, if it's not addressed to that machine, it is passed on to the next machine. If the relayed message is blank, a machine can insert its own message. The ring does not have the problem of simultaneous transmission since information can only be sent when a station receives an empty message unit. The protocol for this system is called *token passing*.

Cabling the Network. Local area network hookups use either coaxial cable or twisted wire pair. Coaxial cable is the type of wire used for cable television. Don't confuse it with television antennae wire. "Coax" has a plastic coated central wire, surrounded by a woven wire shield covered with plastic. Individual computers are attached to this central cable by a T-connector. Systems using coaxial cable can handle data transfer rates of 1 million to 10 million bits per second. Let's see: using an 8-bit byte or character and a 1,500 character page means that this type of network can transfer a hundred pages a second! That's pretty fast compared to phone lines that can take more than eight seconds to send a single page.

Twisted wire pair is the least expensive way of connecting a network. The wire is the same as that used by a normal telephone. Twisted pair networks have a capacity of 100,000 to 1 million bps. For comparison purposes, a measly hundred thousand bps network has a greater capacity than 80 telephone lines connected by 1,200 bps modems.

Using a LAN. A word processor attached to a local area network (LAN) operates like a stand alone word processor. But there'll probably be no disk drives on the machine itself. Instead of the floppy disk drives, there are communal hard disk drive units connected to the network by a special interface unit called a *device server*. When you decide to save or edit a text file, you enter the standard word processor based command; the network controller interprets your request and sends it out over the network to the file server, which establishes the communication link to either save your file to or send it from the central disk.

If you want to send a message, a file, or some electronic mail to someone on the network, you just enter the person's name or device address, and off it goes. If they are on the network they will be told there is a message for them. If they are not on the network your message will be stored and, as soon as they turn on their system, they'll be notified there's a message waiting for them.

Networking in the Home

The networking descriptions so far all send digital on-off pulses to transfer information, which is called *baseband*. There's another type of network, the one used by the cable TV industry, which is capable of transferring information at speeds as high as 100 megabits per second. This technology brings all those television channels into your home. The same TV cable can be used to transmit digital information. It is this type of network that will let you shop and bank from a small terminal or computer in your home. It is also the gateway for your accessing vast information resources at rapid speeds. (By the way, the term *gateway* is used to indicate the interconnection of multiple networks.) It is this type of a network, called *broadband,* that enables information to be sent in the form of words, pictures and sound.

The Future Is Almost Now

The technology of personal computers and word processors makes quantum leaps every year. It seems as if any given system becomes obsolete within two years. Manufacturers announce new models every six months to a year. In many cases the older models are still sufficient, but the new features always seem to clear up so many of the little problems that we've lived with and hated for so long. I trade machines just about every year, and am still always six months behind.

Let me now tell you about some existing technological advances that will be incorporated into machines—probably by the time you purchase this book.

Video Screens

There is a new generation of flat screens that is leading to smaller and lighter television sets as well as to a whole new computer display technology. These screens and the smaller micro floppy disk drives herald a series of briefcase computers with all the features of the present day larger, heavier machines. These systems have the computer and the disk drives right in the computer keyboard. As a matter of fact, the whole computer will be in the keyboard, with either a small scale (several lines of text) or large scale (full page pop-up) display for reviewing and reading text. The briefcase systems being sold as I write this display eight lines of text and don't have disk drives. They sell for about $800. Next year, the same unit with a disk drive should be $800 to $1,000.

Disk and Other Storage Media

The trend in disk storage is toward higher capacity on smaller disks. Floppy disk drives with storage capacity in the megabyte region will become fairly common as a standard option on most systems. Disk capacities keep increasing, while disk size keeps decreasing. Three and one-half inch removable hard disk systems will be available on the $2,000 computer systems in the next couple of years. In addition, solid state devices such as *bubble memory* and what are called RAM disks will increase the access speed for external storage devices. For individuals requiring trillions of bytes of information, the technology of the home video disc players will be integrated with the small computer systems to enable you to access large amounts of information, with pictures and music when needed.

Processors and Things

The 8-bit systems will become the consumer model computers, or home computers as they are presently called. These will become as common as Instamatic cameras, doing all the things that 8-bit machines do, with the added capability of game playing. Interfaces will be available to control appliances and set thermostats in the home. Prices will stay where they are now in the $300 to $1,000 range, but the machines will come with a lot more in the way of peripheral devices and software.

The standard for the professional or personal computer will center around the 16-bit processor chips with user memories in the range of 250K to 1 meg. The software trend for these machines is moving toward integrated systems which allow the combination of multiple applications. This means combining graphics, sketches and calculation spreadsheets with word processing text. All this is possible now, but requires extremely awkward procedures. The software systems are becoming more and more tool-like and easier to use.

The dot matrix printer is not only going to become more intelligent but its character definition will become better. The new models will definitely replace the fully-formed daisy wheel printers.

The Fifth Generation

There is talk of a *fifth generation* of computers which incorporates what is known as "artificial intelligence" into the computer system. This coming generation of machines promises to go beyond any tools that mankind has ever seen before. These will not only assist you in figuring out how *they* work, but will also evaluate the way *you* work, and try to become more useful to your work habits.

To give you an example of how artificial intelligence machines will change things, *think* about how it would be if you had an intelligent lawnmower—a lawnmower that you could tell to go out and mow the lawn, and it would do it. First, it would look very different from the lawnmowers we are accustomed to. The classic lawnmower was designed with very large blades or rotors to minimize the amount of work we people had to do while mowing a lawn. With an intelligent mower, the blades could be made very small. In the morning before going off to work you would send the mower out to graze. It would run around your lawn according to its programmed instructions. In the evening when you returned home the lawn would be mowed.

The impact of fifth generation computers will make drastic changes in the look and operation of many of our tools. They will have voice recognition, which means we can start talking to them or dictating our words, rather than using a keyboard. (Don't get too excited about this one without recalling how difficult it is to get someone to scratch your back in the exact place that it itches!) Pointing can be worth a thousand words. And so we will see a slew of touch-sensitive screens and devices to facilitate cursor movement.

Systems that talk to us already exist, and this will become a great option for those of us who get lonely while working in the middle of the night.

Read that back to me again.

APPENDIX I   Glossary

Acoustic Coupler. An electronic device that converts data signals into tones that can be transmitted over the phone lines using standard telephones. It contains a place to set the telephone handset once the phone connection is made.

Alphanumeric. A term used to describe the combination of alphabetic (A-Z) and numeric (0-9) information.

Application Program. Converts a computer into a tool. It's the reason you purchased a computer in the first place.

Arithmetic Capability. The ability of a word processor to do arithmetic. Important if things like budgets or tables must be typed.

ASCII. Electronic standard for transmitting text. The computer version of Morse code. ASCII stands for American Standard Code for Information Interchange.

Assembler. A computer program that translates assembly language programs into machine language.

Asynchronous Communication. A mode of transmitting data one character at a time between a computer or word processor and a printer, or between two computers. The most common means of communication between computing machines.

Auto Answer Modem. A modem capable of answering the phone.

Automatic Carriage Return. A feature that lets you type without slowing down at the end of the line. If a word extends into the right margin it is automatically moved to the next line. Also called *wordwrap*.

Backup. To make copies of important documents or files on either diskettes or tape. This enables recreation of the files if the originals are lost, stolen or damaged.

Baseband. A network using a single digital signal for communication.

Basic. A programming language using algebraic-like statements.

Bidirectional Printing. A means of increasing printing speed by printing odd lines going from left to right and even lines from right to left.

Bisynchronous. A synchronous half-duplex protocol for data transmission on IBM mainframes (whew!).

Bit. The basic unit of information for storing and transmitting data. Short for binary digit. Always has a 0 or 1 "state."

Bit Rate. Rate at which bits are transferred over a communication line (speed in bits per second).

Boiler Plate. Portions of text stored on disk that are used continually with little modification to create standard documents containing customized information.

Bold Print. The over-printing of a portion of text to cause it to stand out from the rest of the page.

Broadband. Transmission over a cable TV type network. Used for very high data rates or to send voice and video as well.

Bubble Memory. Recent technical development for storing large amounts of information. It's slower than RAM memory but faster than disk.

Bulletin Board. A communications program facilitating the sending and storing of programs and information.

Bus. The path for information transfer within a computer or word processor. *Data bus* transfers one word at a time.

Byte. Unit of computer storage equivalent to one character or eight bits.

Camera Ready Copy. Output from a word processor or phototypesetter ready to be used for offset printing.

Capacity. The number of characters that can be stored on a diskette or the document size that can be worked on in the machine. Capacity is usually expressed in *bytes* or *characters* of storage.

Carriage Return. The key on the keyboard that indicates the end of a line and causes cursor movement to the left margin of the next line.

Cassette. Resembles an audio magnetic tape cassette. Used for data and program storage.

Center. The equal positioning of text on both sides of a centerline between two margins.

Character Generation. The method used to create characters, composed of a series of dots, on the display screen or printer.

Character. A single piece of printed information. The character alphabet consists of letters (A-Z), numbers (0-9), and special symbols (:,/[]—).

Character Oriented Word Processor. A word processor capable of printing a variable number of different characters on a line. Character oriented word processors will do *proportional printing*.

Character Set. Total number of different characters displayable on a word processor. This includes upper and lower case alphabet, numbers and special symbols.

Clear Key. The key used to cancel an operation that has already been started, to cancel a delete operation or to stop printing.

Coaxial Cable. Cable with a single center wire surrounded by a braided wire shield. Used for connecting terminals, computers, and word processors for high-speed communication.

COBOL. *Common Business Oriented Language.* COBOL is to business programming what Hebrew is to religion.

Compiler. A program used to translate higher level language instructions into machine language.

Computer. An electronic machine that can be converted into a useful tool by a program. It's also the physical machine used for word processing.

Conditional Sale. A lease arrangement in which the customer owns the equipment at the end of the lease period. Available as a means of obtaining equipment with minimal cash outlay and maximum tax reduction.

Contention Protocol. Means of resolving the competition between several computing devices attempting to access a computer network.

Continuous Form Paper. Perforated paper normally fan-folded to facilitate automatic paper feed to a printer. (After printing the pages can be easily separated.)

Control. A character that initiates a machine operation (it doesn't print).

Control Code Printout. A printout indicating the normally non-printed control characters.

Copy. The process of copying a file from one physical disk to another.

CP/M. *Control Program for Microcomputers.* Developed by Digital Research, it is the most popular operating system for small-scale computers.

CPS. *Characters Per Second.* The speed at which a printer can print.

CPU. *Central Processing Unit.* The heart of a computer, it controls the interpretation and execution of instructions.

Create. The process of telling the system that a new document or data base will be entered. The system creates space for it on the disk.

CRT. *Cathode Ray Tube.* The TV-like screen used by the word processor to display information as it is typed and the means by which the system writes messages to you.

Cursor. The means of indicating the present position on the CRT, usually a blinking square or underline. It is moved around the screen by the directional arrow keys.

Daisy Wheel. The print element used in letter-quality printers. The daisy wheel has a raised character on each "petal" and is rotated to print letters.

Data Base Manager. An applications program used to organize information for easy access.

Data Compression. A technique to reduce the disk storage space required by text or program files.

Data Processing. The use of a computer to work with numbers. Usually refers to business or commercial applications.

Data Rate. Rate at which data is transferred on a communication line.

Delete. The editing operation to remove characters, words, lines and paragraphs from text. Once the section is deleted the rest of the text closes up.

Dictionary. A program used to help you correct spelling errors while editing a document.

Directory. A list of all files and programs stored on a disk.

Disk Drive. A storage device for holding electronic representation of text, programs, or of data files capable of random access.

Diskette (or Floppy Disk). Magnetic coated flexible plastic disk able to store 100,000 to one million characters of information. Disk sizes are standard 8", mini 5¼" and micro 3" to 4".

Document. The name given to any text material written and stored on a word processor.

Dot Matrix. A method of generating display or printed characters formed by a grid of dots.

Dot Matrix Printer. A printer which fires pins against a print ribbon to create a character made up of dots.

Double Spacing. Skipping a blank line after each line of text, used often for draft copy printing because it leaves room to write in corrections.

Dumb Terminal. A terminal that can only send and receive information. A "smart" terminal has processing and storage capability as well.

Echo Mode. Computer-to-computer communication in which one of the machines echoes received information back to the other. It is used to ensure that keyboard-entered information has been received correctly.

Edit. Changing the contents of a document by adding, removing, or rearranging text.

Electronic Mail. The transfer of documents over an electronic network to another word processor or computer.

Elite Type. A type face printed in 12 characters per inch. Also called *twelve pitch*.

Encryption. Coding information for security purposes.

Enter. A key on the word processor that instructs it to carry out an instruction. Also, to type in information on the keyboard.

Ergonomics. Design of equipment for user comfort and safety.

Escape. A key on a word processor that lets you cancel an instruction that is underway.

Field. A unit of information within a record.

File. A collection of documents stored on a disk.

Floppy. See *Diskette*.

Flush Left. Text lines aligned on the left margin. Also called *left justified*.

Flush Right. Text lines aligned along the right margin. Also called *right justified*.

Font. The type style available for printing (description of style and size).

Footer. A line of information printed on the *bottom* of each page of a multipage document.

Format. The complete printed form that a document will take.

Formatting. The "initializing" of a disk for use by a computer system. Formatting a disk erases all information that was on a disk.

Fourth Generation Language. A program that converts a computer into a useful tool for non-programmers.

Friction Feed. A means of feeding single pages to a printer by friction rollers, in contrast to a *sprocket drive*.

Full Duplex. Data transmission over a communication line in both directions at the same time.

Full Page Display. A CRT display of a full page of material, normally 66-100 characters wide by 54-66 characters long.

Function Keys. Additional keyboard keys for carrying out special word processing functions.

Gateway. Equipment designed to connect two or more dissimilar networks.

General Ledger. An accounting program for keeping track of day-to-day business earnings and expenses.

Ghost Hyphen. Hyphens placed in words that are only printed if the word falls at the end of a line.

Half Duplex. Data transmission over a communication line in one direction at a time.

Hard Copy. Text printed on paper.

Hard Disk. A high capacity data storage device capable of storing megabytes of information.

Hardware. Physical computer equipment. The stuff you can touch: VDT, computer disk drives, printer, etc.

Header. A line of information printed at the top of each page.

Highlight. A means of emphasizing a portion of text by outlining or reversing the video image.

Horizontal Scrolling. Ability to move text horizontally across the screen to work on documents whose width is greater than the screen width.

Hyphenation. Division of a word at the end of a line by inserting a hyphenation mark at the end of a syllable.

Illumination. The overall light level in a space, measured in foot-candles.

Impact Printer. Any printer that forms a character by forcing an imprint mechanism (such as a key) against a ribbon and onto the paper.

Information Processing. Combining word processing and data processing into a single system.

Information Utility. A paid subscription service providing access to large scale data bases and other computer facilities.

Ink Jet Printer. A non-impact printer that shoots small droplets of ink at the paper to create characters.

Insert. An editing operation in which additional text elements are added into a document.

Install. Process of modifying a program to work with a terminal or printer.

Intercharacter Spacing. The spacing between characters, a fixed value for all printers except *proportional* ones in which the spacing varies with the size and shape of the character printed.

Interword Spacing. For *justified* printing the spacing between words on a line is varied to ensure that the characters align with both the left and right margins.

Justification. The alignment of all text lines so that they are flush with both the left and right margins. See also *flush left* and *flush right*.

Keyboard. Part of a word processor that looks like a typewriter containing electronic keys for entering information. Word processor keyboards usually contain more keys than a typewriter keyboard.

LAN. *Local Area Network.* A communications network operating in a limited area.

Lease Purchase Plan. See *Conditional Sale*.

Letter Quality Printer. High quality printer that creates printed copy as good as that produced on an electric typewriter.

Line Oriented Word Processor. The standard word processor that lets you create text having a typewriter look. It is not capable of proportional printing.

LPM. The speed of a printer, measured in Lines Per Minute (See also CPS.)

Lumination. The light level reflected from or emitted from a surface.

Margin. The boarder around a printed page: left, right, top and bottom.

Mega. One million. Ten megabytes of storage can hold 10 million characters of information.

Menu. A means to choose between available alternatives. Usually displayed as a numbered list.

Microcomputer. A small-scale computer that can be used for word processing. The most popular and least expensive are the 8 and 16 bit machines.

Micro Diskette. A 4'' or smaller disk capable of storing 200,000 to 500,000 characters of information.

Mini Diskette. A 5¼'' diskette capable of storing 100,000 to 1 million characters of information.

Modem. Also known as a *data set*. Enables computers and word processors to communicate over telephone lines.

MS DOS. The standard operating system for the 16 bit IBM personal computer.

Multitasking. A computer or word processor with an operating system capable of running multiple programs at the same time.

Multiuser. A multitasking system working with several people at the same time.

OEM. *Original Equipment Manufacturer* of a word processor system or one of its component parts.

One Line Display. A single line display setup usually found on electronic typewriters.

Operating System. The control program that handles all ''housekeeping'' functions required by the word processing program. It's your behind-the-scenes technical crew. Operating systems can be single user, multiuser, or multitasking for a single user.

Optical Character Reader (OCR). A device that reads printed or typed material, converting it into electronic editable word processor form.

Orphan. A single line that is the first line of a paragraph located as the last line of a page. Considered poor typographic placement, it is corrected by adjusting the page break so that the line is moved to the next page and becomes the first line of the first paragraph.

Overstrike. Printing over a character with the same or a different character.

Page. The amount of text on a single sheet of paper. Generally estimated as 1500 characters.

Page Scrolling. A feature that lets the system move forward or backward through a document one page at a time.

Paragraph. A section of text usually set off by an entered carriage return, with indentation or extra line space before its first line.

Parallel Port. Used for intermachine communication where one byte or word is sent at a time.

Peripheral. Any device that is attached to the word processor. Printers, disk drives and modems are peripherals.

Personality Area. The memory area of the computer that holds the *application program*. If the application program is a word processor, the machine assumes the personality of a writing machine.

Photocomposition. A process for producing *camera-ready copy*, which includes multiple character fonts and sizes. The copy is created by a keyboard and use of a graphic display screen, plus a projected optical process.

Pica Type. A print size of 10 characters per inch. Also called *ten pitch*.

Pin Feed. Printer paper movement relying on special holes in the paper that fit a turning ring of pins on the machine.

Pitch. The number of printed characters per inch. Ten pitch is called *Pica;* twelve pitch is called *Elite*.

Plasma Display. A very thin, non-CRT text display screen.

Port. Physical place where information enters or leaves a computer.

Preview. The display of text on a CRT as it will appear on paper.

Printer. A device used to print text on paper.

Print Wheel. See *Daisy Wheel*.

Program. A set of instructions, stored in the *program storage memory area*, which establishes the system "personality." It converts a computer into a useful tool.

Program Storage Area. The portion of the computer's memory that holds and runs the *application program*.

Prompts. Short messages to assist the operator in what to do next.

Proportional Printing. The width and spacing of characters results in hard copy that is very print like. Both the software and the printer must support this feature.

Protocol. The formal control information required to make it possible for two word processors or computers to communicate with each other. It's a set of rules for the exchange of information.

Ragged Right. Printed output with the type aligned flush with the left side margins only. An alternative to justified text.

RAM. *Random Access Memory*. A measure of the internal computer storage space available for the word processor program and text. Specified in *kilobytes*, otherwise known as thousands of characters.

Record. An item of stored information composed of a series of fields.

Reformat. The process of re-establishing margins, etc., after changes are made to a document.

Rename. To change the name of a stored document on a disk.

Rent Purchase Plan. A rental agreement in which a percentage of monthly rental payments can be applied to equipment purchase.

Replace. Replacement of characters or words of text with new text.

Reset. A button to restart the system. Creates a memory blank out.

Reverse Video. Display of text in reverse colors for emphasis. If the screen is displaying text in white on black, highlighted portions would be in black on white.

Revision. Making changes to a document stored on a disk *file*.

Ribbon. Inked cloth or carbon film used to create printed image on paper.

Ring. A *comunication network* in which all terminals are connected in a loop arrangement.

ROM. *Read Only Memory.* A portion of memory where programs and control information is stored.

RS-232. A common type of connection for attaching word processors to printers, terminals and other computers.

Scrolling. Means of viewing more of a document than will fit in the CRT "window" at one time. The text is scrolled both horizontally and vertically.

Search. To locate a character, word or series of words in a document. The search starts from the current position and will move toward the end of the document, stopping when a match is found.

Search and Replace. The process of finding indicated text and replacing it with alternate text.

Serial. A method of communication with a printer or terminal in which a single bit of information is sent at a time. *Parallel* communication sends one character at a time.

Shared Logic. A word processing setup where more than one person is using the same computer system from different video display terminals.

Shared Resource. A word processing system where several terminals or word processors share peripherals (non-computer parts) such as the printer and disk storage.

Sheet Feeder. A printer attachment to feed single pages to a printer.

Software. Programs that establish the machine personality. Programs are kept on the systems disk and loaded into the computer program area or personality area for use.

Spread Sheet. A program that transforms a computer into a tool for entering, editing, storing and doing arithmetic calculations with rows of numbers.

Stand Alone System. A complete word processor containing a VDT, small computer, printer, and word processing program.

Super Micro. A microcomputer using a 16 or 32 bit processor.

Synchronous. A communication made between word processors in which data are transmitted as blocks of characters.

Telecommunications. Communication between word processors using the telephone lines.

Terminal. See VDT.

Text Editing. A program for working with written text. Originally it referred to programs for revising computer programs, but recently has become synonymous with word processing.

Thermal Printer. A non-impact printer which uses heat sensitive paper.

Time Sharing. The sharing of power and cost of large computer facilities among a number of word processing or computer terminals.

True Lease. A lease arrangement in whch the ownership of the equipment remains with the lessor. This makes monthly payments a tax deductable expense.

Unix. The most widely used minicomputer multiuser operating system.

Utilities. Programs used to perform support operations for auxiliary disk functions. Copying disks for *backup* is a utility function.

VDT. *Video Display Terminal* A combination video display screen and keyboard.

Vendor. A company that supplies word processing equipment or supplies.

Volume. An item of magnetic storage containing a directory of files stored on it.

Widow. A short portion of a paragraph ending line of text appearing on the top of a new page. It can be corrected by rearranging the page format to move it back to the previous page.

Winchester Disk. A rigid, non-removable sealed magnetic disk unit, more compact and reliable than floppys. Capable of storing 5-100 megabytes of information.

Word. The machine *word size* is the amount of information that can be transferred in one chunk. It is usually a whole number of bytes.

Word Processing System. The hardware, software and procedures used to carry out writing, editing, and filing text.

Word Wrap. The automatic movement of text exceeding the right margin to the next line during typing. Increases typing speed since margin decisions are made automatically by the system.

Work Station. An individual work area for carrying out word processing, consisting of the word processor, desk, chair and peripheral equipment.

APPENDIX II: Word Processor Purchase Checklists

Using the Checklists

These checklists were created to give you a handle on available word processor features. Go through the lists and check off all the features that are important to the type of writing you'll be doing. These are the features that will define your system. While shopping for your word processor go through the checklist with the sales people so you can find out what features each of the systems you're considering has. You might just have the sales person initial the filled in checklist before you actually purchase the system. That way, if he inadvertently told you his system had features that it doesn't, you have some recourse.

Use the list to help you organize and keep track of the features each system has and doesn't have. Don't put down dollars for any system until you have compared its features to your requirements and at least one other system.

The Word Processing Software Checklist

Here I line up the various features and options available in word processing programs. Remember, these functions are separate from computer hardware. (If you are considering a machine that only does word processing, or a personal computer that is supplied with a word processing program, it is even *more* important to separate the software from the hardware.)

An L is used to indicate functions found in low priced word processors (less than $150), an M for medium ($150-500), and an H for the high priced (greater than $500) programs. Remember, these features are *not* qualities of the hardware—the computer, printer, or disk drives.

General Features

1) Quality of user and instruction manuals
   Are they written in English?
   Is there an index and table of contents?
   Are there good examples?
2) Menu driven options for use (M)
   Menu removable for more advanced user (M)
3) Edits programs as well as text (L)
4) Prints one file while editing another (M)
5) Largest size file that can be worked with: 10, 20, 30, over 30 pages
6) Error-handling quality of error messages
7) Do/undo while editing—the whoops key (H)
8) Contains definable function keys (H)
9) Number of keystrokes for routine commands
10) Is the word processor *Character Oriented* (supports multiple character sizes in the same line as well as proportional printing)? (H)
11) Text storage capacity is limited by available disk storage rather than the computer memory (M)

Text Entry and Editing

1) Automatic carriage return or wordwrap (L)
   Word wrap override (M)
2) Delete Options: char   line   word   sent   para   page   block   screen
   Delete and restore (H)
   Delete columns for table entry (H)
   Delete from cursor to the end of text (L)
   Delete from cursor to beginning of text (L)
3) Insert
   Typeover (L)
   Text open (M)
   Push ahead (L)
   Insert columns (H)
   Block move and copy (Cut & Paste) (l)
       Maximum size block that can be inserted or moved
4) Search and Replace (L)
   Find and replace a number of times (L)
   Repeat operation (L)
   Find and replace backwards (M)
   Whole words only (M)
   Lower and upper case distinction (M)
5) Tabs—Settings for:
   Decimal (M)
   Flush left (L)
   Flush right (H)
   Centered (H)
   Set by cursor (L)
   Set by command (L)

Text Formatting

Margin Setting: top, bottom, left, right (L)
Line spacing: single, double, triple (L)
Lines per page (L)
Temporary margins and indenting (M)
Right justification (L)
Left justification (L)
Center text (L)
Automatic reform after insert or delete (M)
Headers and footers (L)
   odd-even page distinction (M)
Page numbering (L)
   automatic numbering (L)
   display during editing (M)
   position top or bottom (L)
   odd-even page distinction (M)
   conditional page for widows and orphans (M)
Hyphenation (I)
   automatic (H)

use of dictionary (H)
prompt in the *hot zone* (L)
automatic hyphen removal (M)
Footnotes: Multiple lines attached to the text (H)

Print Functions

Character size and styles: pica, elite, micro (M)
Underline (M)
Boldface (M)
Subscript (M)
Superscript (M)
Ribbon color change (M)
Print text while editing (M)
Reverse printer line feed (M)
Proportional printing (M)
Space justified printing (text aligned by adding partial spaces between words) (M)
Print portions of the text (M)
Print in Draft Mode (M)

Cursor Movement

Up/down/left/right (L)
Movement by: word/sentence/line/paragraph (M)
Movement by screen and page (H)
Move to beginning or end of text (L)
Move to place marker (M)
Scroll for pages wider than the screen (L)

Files

Display file directory (M)
Delete files (M)
Rename files (M)
Automatic backup (M)
Read another file and place at the present cursor position (M)
Write part of document to another text file name (M)
File name size more than eight characters (H)
File descriptors available (H)
File search (H)
Sorting capability (H)
Store as data and print files (M)
View another file while editing (M)

Screen appearance

Text is displayed as it will be printed (M)
Status line to indicate page number, column position and functions in use
Cursor quality—inverse video, light square, underline
How are special functions indicated on the screen? For example, boldface and
   superscripts.

Display multiple character sizes
Display proportional print

Hardware Checklist

This checklist contains functions of the computer or word processor hardware: the physical machines including the computer, printer and disk drives. I have also included the *operating system* in this section since this is usually supplied with the computer or wordprocessor.

Keyboard:

Touch: good? ok? poor?
Repeating keys?
Keys sculpted to fingers?
Matte surface color to avoid glare?
Number of special function keys: fixed   user definable
Keyboard moveable and attached by at least 3 ft. cord?
Keyboard weight heavy enough to be stable?
Is key arrangement convenient?

Display Screen:

Does the screen have anti-glare coating?
Character height large enough to read?
Character dot resolution 7 x 9 or better?
Space between characters sufficient for readibility?
Highlighting text: *inverse video* or contrast change?
Cursor visibility: blinking character or underline?
Multiple character sizes available?
Display color: white, green or amber?
Is the screen flicker perceivable?
Contrast and brightness adjustable?
Is the screen tiltable and adjustable?

Computer or central processor:

8 bit, 16 bit, 32 bit, or greater?
Available computer memory greater than 48,000 bytes (characters)?
Is operating system standard CP/M, Unix, MS-DOS?
Capable of supporting multiple stations?   How many?
Run in shared resource mode?
Other software available?

Disk Storage (formatted):

Standard: 8''   250k   500k   1meg (150-600 pages)
Winchester disk: 2meg   5meg   100meg (1200-6,000 pages)
Capacity: 200k,   400k,   800k,   greater? (150k = 100 pages)
Standard, Mini, Micro?
Hard disk available?

Capacity: 5, 10 or greater (megabytes)?
Removable or fixed disk?
Backup Medium: disk, streaming tape or video tape?

Printers (all):

Speed (characters per second)
Number of available fonts
Incremental spacing in 1/120 of an inch
Horizontal spacing in 1/48 of an inch
Proportional printing
Draft mode for speed
Graphics capability
Half line forward/backward for super and subscripts?
Maximum page width
Single sheet feed
Envelope feed
Ease of changing ribbon
Ease of changing paper
Adjustable tractors for paper feed
Multiple color ribbon
Noise level

Impact Printers (letter quality)—
Daisy wheel or thimble
Speed: 15cps   30cps   55cps
Print quality
Ease of changing wheels
Will hold more than one wheel?
Printer intelligence: automatic margins and spacing
Is it precision (capable of incremental spacing)?

Dot Matrix—
Resolution: 7x9   9x9   9x24   better
Print quality
How many character sizes and print styles are available?
Print speed: 50   100   200cps
Tab setting
Printer intelligence (automatic margins and spacing, proportional printing)

Non Impact—
Ink Jet
Print quality
Print speed
Number of type fonts
Thermal Printer
Dot resolution
On line character sizes
Speed
Cost of paper

APPENDIX III: Resources

Software and Hardware Suppliers

Here are lists of companies that sell software and hardware products applicable to small computer word processing. The listing of a company isn't meant to be an endorsement of either the company or their products. I have included the names of companies that people frequently talk about. My apologies to the hundreds of companies that have fine products and were not included here.

If you plan to phone any of the companies I suggest you check with *800 information* (800-555-1212) to see if they have a toll free number. I make it a point to check for 800 numbers whenever I have to phone a large company long distance.

Software Sources—Word Processing

The word processing programs listed in this section fall into the middle range cost and feature category. They can be run under most personal computer operating systems. I have not included prices which tend to change like the weather.

Easy Writer
Information Unlimited
281 Arlington Ave.
Kensington, CA 94707

Final Word
Mark of the Unicorn
PO Box 423
Arlington, MA 02174

Word Processing
INBI Incorporated
1695 38th Street
Boulder, CO 80300

PALANTIER
Designer Software
3400 Montrose Blvd.
Houston, TX 77006

Peach Text
Peach Tree Software Inc.
3 Corporate Square
Atlanta, GA 30329

Perfect Writer
Perfect Software
1400 Shattuck Ave.
Berkeley, CA 94709

Scriptsit
Radio Shack
PO Box 2910
Fort Worth, TX 76101

Select
Select Information Systems
919 Sir Francis Drake Blvd.
Kentfield, CA 94904

Spellbinder
Lexisoft Inc.
PO Box 267
Davis, CA 95616

Volkswriter
Lifetree Software
411 Pacific
Monterey, CA 93940

Wordstar
MicroPro
1299 4th Street
San Rafael, CA 94901

Software—Spelling Checkers and Dictionaries

The following companies market and sell auxiliary programs that work with most of the word processor created text files to assist with the checking and correcting of spelling. The price range is $50 to $200.

Easy Spell
IUS
2401 Morinship Way
Sausalito, CA 93614

Spell
Software Toolworks
14478 Gloriette Drive
Sherman Oaks, CA 91423

Electronic Webster
Cornucopia Software
PO Box 5028
Walnut Creek, CA 94596

SpellGuard
ISA
915 Timothy Lane
Menlo Park, CA 94025

Electronic Thesaurus
Dictronics
362 Fifth Ave.
New York, NY 10001

Spell Star
MicroPro International
1299 4th Street
San Rafael, CA 94901

Proofreader
Aspen Software
PO Box 14
Tijeras, NM 87059

The Word Plus
Oasis Systems
2765 Reynard Way
San Diego, CA 92103

Software—Calculation Spreadsheets

Here are programs that will convert your computer into an accountant. Some of the programs work as just spreadsheets while others will also do graphics, some database management and a little word processing.

MBA
Context Management Systems
23844 Hawthorne Blvd.
Torrance, CA 90505

Perfect Calc
Perfect Software
702 Harrison St.
Berkeley, CA 94710

MicroPlan
Chang Labs
5300 Stevens Creek Blvd.
San Jose, CA 95129

Super Calc
Sorcim Corporation
2310 Lundy Ave.
San Jose, CA 95050

Multiplan
MicroSoft
10700 Northrup Way
Bellevue, WA 98004

Visicalc
Visicorp Inc.
2895 Zanker Rd.
San Jose, CA 95134

1-2-3
Lotus
55 Wheeler St.
Cambridge, MA 02138

Software—Data Base Management Systems

These data base management systems will run on most small computers:

Condor
Condor Computer Corporation
PO Box 8318
Ann Arbor, MI 48107

Personal Pearl
Relational Systems International
PO Box 12892
Salem, OR 97309

dBase II
Ashton-Tate
9929 West Jefferson Blvd.
Culver City, CA 90230

Select II
Micro-Applications
7033 Village Parkway
Dublin, CA 94566

MDBS III
ISE International
350 West Sagmore St.
West Lafayette, IN 47906

Business Software Vendors

Planning on computerizing your business? Here are a few companies that sell software for business accounting:

BPI Systems, Inc.
3423 Guadalupe Rd.
Austin, TX 78705

Lifeboat Associates
1650 Third Ave.
New York, NY 10028

Business Applications Software
16755 Littlefield Lane
Los Gatos, CA 95030

Peachtree Software
3445 Peachtree Rd.
Atlanta, GA 30326

Charles Mann & Associates
55722 Santa Fe Trail
Yucca Valley, CA 92284

Spokane Micro Computer
13210 Mill Road
Spokane, WA 99218

Computer Systems Design
1105 W. Lincoln
PO Box 735
Yakima, WA 98907

Structured Systems Group
5204 Claremont
Oakland, CA 94618

CYMA Corporation
2160 East Brown Rd.
Mesa, AZ 85203

Taranto and Associates
PO Box 6073
San Rafael, CA 94903

Datasmith
PO Box 8036
Shawnee Mission, KS 66208

Targhee Software Engineering
370 East South Temple
Salt Lake City, Utah 84111

Digital Technology
Box 178590
San Diego, CA 92117

Systems Software

These organizations market the most popular operating systems for small computers and word processors:

Bell Laboratories (UNIX)
150 JGR
Short Hills, NJ 07078

Microsoft (MS-DOS, XENIX)
10700 Northrup Way
Bellevue, WA 98004

Digital Research (CP/M)
160 Central
Pacific Grove, CA 93950

Softech Microsystems Inc. (P-System)
9494 Black Mountain Road
San Diego, CA 92126

Communications Software

These outfits sell communications software that runs on a variety of machines under several operating systems. Price range is $50 to $150.

ASCOM
Dynamic Microprocessor Associates
545 Fifth Ave.
New York, NY 10017

Lync
International Software Alliance
1835 Mission Ridge Rd.
Santa Barbara, CA 93103

CLINK
Westico
25 Van Fant St.
Norwalk, CT 06855

Micromodem
First Software
5622 East Presido
Scottsdale, AZ 85254

CrossTalk
Microstuff Inc.
1845 The Exchange
Atlanta, GA 30339

Mite
Mycroft Labs Inc.
Post Office Box 6045
Tallahassee, FL 32301

Data Capture
Southeastern Software
7743 Briarwood Drive
New Orleans, LA 70128

Smartcom
Hayes Microcomputer Products
5923 Peachtree Industrial Blvd.
Norcross, GA 30092

LogOn
Ferox Microsystems Inc.
1701 N. Fort Meyer Drive
Arlington, VA 22209

Telios
Genasys
11820 Parklawn Dr.
Rockville, MD 20852

Hardware Manufacturers

At latest count, there are over 500 companies selling more than 1,400 different machines billed as word processors or that can be used for word processing. I have broken the listings up according to machine categories, but listed each manufacturer just once, even though many of them sell equipment that could be placed in more than one of the lists. Use the lists mainly as a starting point.

Stand Alone Word Processors

These are the best, most flexible and most costly of all the word processing systems. The systems usually come complete with hardware, software, and in many cases a printer. Here's where to start your word processor search. Check the Yellow Pages of your phone book for the nearest representative or write the central office listed here:

A.B. Dick
570 West Touhy
Niles, IL 60848

A.M. Jacquard Systems
PO Box 604
Inglewood, CA 90312

CompuCorp
2211 Michigan Ave.
Santa Monica, CA 90404

C.P.T. Corporation
8100 Mitchell Road
PO Box 295
Minneapolis, MN 55440

Datapoint Corporation
9725 Datapoint Drive
San Antonio, TX 78284

Digital Equipment Corporation
Word Processing Group
4 Continental Blvd.
Merrimack, NH 03054

Exxon Office Systems
777 Long Ridge Road
Stamford, CT 06904

Honeywell Information Systems
200 Smith Street
Waltham, MA 02154

IBM
Office Products Division
Parsons Pond Road
Franklin Lakes, NH 07417

Lanier Business Products
1700 Chantilly Drive N.E.
Atlanta, GA 30324

Lexitron
1840 DeHavilland Drive
Thousand Oaks, CA 91359

NBI
1695 38th Street
Boulder, CO 80301

Phillips Information Systems
4040 McEwen Drive
Dallas, TX 75234

Xerox Corporation
Office Systems Division
11 West Mockingbird Lane
Dallas, TX 75247

Portable Computers

Portable computers are generally the least expensive machines you can buy. The purchase price usually includes one of the word processing and spreadsheet programs listed in the software section. By the way, the word "portable" in the computer world refers to machines weighing 30 pounds or less. The only thing required in addition to one of these machines is a printer.

Casio Inc.
15 Gardner Road
Fairfield, NJ 07006

Compact Computer Corp.
12330 Perry Road
Houston, TX 70070

Corona Data Systems
31324 Via Collins, Suite 10
Westlake Village, CA 91361

Epson America
3215 Kashiwa Street
Torrance, CA 90505

Gavilon Computer Corp.
240 Hacienda Ave.
Campbell, CA 95008

Grid Systems
2535 Garcia Ave.
Mountain View, CA 94043

Hewlett Packard
1000 Circle Road
Corvallis, OR 97330

Nonlinear Systems
533 Stevens Ave.
Solano Beach, CA 92075

Osborne Computer Corp.
26500 Corporate Ave.
Hayward, CA 94545

Otrona Advanced Systems
4755 Walnut Ave.
Boulder, CO 80301

Panasonic Company
One Panasonic Way
Secausus, NJ 07094

Radio Shack-Tandy Corp.
One Tandy Center
Fort Worth, TX 76102

SEEQUA Computer Corp.
209 West Street
Annapolis, MD 21401

Sharp Electronics
10 Sharp Plaza
Paramus, NJ 07662

Telcon Industries Inc.
1401 N.W. 69th Street
Fort Lauderdale, FL 33309

Personal Computers

These machines usually include the computer and a keyboard. You will likely have to purchase a video monitor or VDT. Depending on where you buy one, it may or may not come with an operating system and word processing software.

Apple Computer
20525 Mariani Ave.
Cupertino, CA 95014

Atari Inc.
1312 Crossman
Sunnyvale, CA 94086

Commodore Business Machines, Inc.
487 Devon Park Drive
Wayne, PA 19087

Dynalogic
141 Bentley Ave.
Ottawa, Ontario, Canada K2E 6T7

Fortune
1501 Industrial Road
San Carlos, CA 94070

Hitachi
401 West Artesia Blvd.
Compton, CA 90220

IBM
PO Box 1328
Boca Raton, FL 33432

Intelligent Systems Corp.
225 Technology Park
Norcross, GA 30092

NEC Information Systems
5 Militia Drive
Lexington, MA 02173

Olivetti
155 White Plains Road
Tarrytown, NY 10591

Sanyo Business Systems
51 Joseph Street
Moonachie, NJ 07074

Sony Microcomputer Products
7 Mercedes Drive
Montvale, NJ 07645

Toshiba America
2441 Michelle Drive
Tustin, CA 92680

Victor Data Products
3900 N. Rockwell Street
Chicago, IL 60618

Multiuser Systems

These companies sell computer systems which can work with more than one person at a time. They come supplied with a fancy multiuser operating system and usually a hard disk for text and data storage.

Altos Computer Systems
2360 Bering Drive
San Jose, CA 95131

Columbia Data Products
8990 Route 108
Columbia, MD 21045

Corvus Systems
2029 O'Toole Ave.
San Jose, CA 95131

Cromemco
280 Bernardo Ave.
Mountainview, CA 94043

Data General Corp.
4400 Computer Drive
Westboro, MA 01580

Digital Equipment Corp.
2 Mount Royal Ave.
Marlboro, MA 01752

Eagle Computer
983 University Ave.
Los Gatos, CA 95030

Fortune Systems
1501 Industrial Road
San Carlos, CA 94070

Hewlett Packard
1000 N.E. Circle Blvd.
Corvallis, OR 97330

Molecular Computer
1841 Zanker Road
San Jose, CA 95112

North Star Computers
1440 Catalina St.
San Leandro, CA 94577

Ohio Scientific
1334 S. Chillicothe
Aura, Ohio 44202

Phase One Systems
7700 Edgewater Drive
Oakland, CA 94621

Radio Shack
1800 One Tandy Center
Forth Worth, TX 76102

Televideo Systems
1170 Morse Ave.
Sunnyvale, CA 94086

Vector Graphic
500 North Ventura Park Rd.
Thousand Oaks, CA 91320

Victor Business Products
3900 N. Rockwell Street
Chicago, IL 60618

Dot Matrix Printers

Dot matrix printers are my favorite type of printer and the better ones can be used in place of a letter quality printer. Here are some people who make them:

Annadex
9825 DeSoto Ave.
Chatsworth, CA 91311

Axiom Corporation
1014 Griswold Ave.
San Fernando, CA 91340

C. Itoh Electronics
5301 Beethoven Street
Los Angeles, CA 90066

Centronics
1 Wall Street
Hudson, NH 03051

Epson America
3415 Kashiwa Street
Torrance, CA 90505

Integral Data Systems
Route 135
Millford, NH 03055

NEC
5 Militia Drive
Lexington, MA 02173

Okidata
11 Gaither Drive
Mt. Laurel, NJ 08054

Panasonic
One Panasonic Way
Secaucus, NJ 07094

Star Micronics
200 Park Ave.
New York, NY 10166

Toshiba America
2441 Michelle Drive
Tustin, CA 92680

Daisy Wheel Printers

The daisy wheel or letter quality printer is sold either as a precision or standard printer. The standard printer types exactly like a typewriter. The precision variety is capable of incremental spacing for proportional printing or better looking print justification.

Precision:

Anderson Jacobson
521 Charcot Ave.
San Jose, CA 95131

Data Products
6200 Canoga Ave.
Woodland Hills, CA 91365

Diablo Systems
24500 Industrial Blvd.
Hayward, CA 94545

NEC Information Systems
5 Militia Drive
Lexington, MA 02173

Pertec Computers
12910 Culver Blvd.
Los Angeles, CA 90066

Qume Corp.
2350 Qume Drive
San Jose, CA 95131

Non-Precision:

Brother International
8 Corporate Place
Ithaca, NY 15850

Bytewriter
125 North View Road
Ithaca, NY 14850

Olivetti
505 White Plains Road
Tarrytown, NY 10591

Smith Corona
65 Locust Ave.
New Canaan, CT 06840

Systemed
PO Box 18
Mountain City, TN 37683

Modems

Your entrance into the world of telecommunications requires a modem. Here are folks who manufacture and sell them:

Anderson Jacobson
25 Olympia Ave.
Wolburn, MA 01801

Bell Telephone
(call your local phone company)

Cermetek Microelectronics
1308 Borregas Ave.
Sunnyvale, CA 94086

Gandolf Data Inc.
1019 South Noel Ave.
Wheeling, IL 60090

Hayes Microcomputer Products
5835 Peachtree Corners East
Norcross, GA 91356

Novation
18664 Oxnard St.
Tarzana, CA 91356

Multitech
82 Second Ave.
New Brighton, MN 55112

Omnitec
2405 South 20 St.
Phoenix, AZ 85023

Racal Vadic
222 Caspian Drive
Sunnyvale, CA 94086

Local Area Networks for Word Processing

These companies sell complete system networks, including personal computers or word processors, or the means to network your own systems together:

Compucorp
2211 Michigan Ave.
Santa Monica, CA 90404

Corvus Systems
2029 O'Toole Ave.
San Jose, CA 95131

Contel Information Systems
130 Steamboat Rd.
Great Neck, LI 10024

Cromemco
280 Bernardo Ave.
Mountain View, CA 94043

Datapoint Corp.
9725 Datapoint Drive
San Antonio, TX 78284

Digital Microsystems
1840 Embarcadero
Oakland, CA 94606

Exo Corporation
1265 Montecito Ave.
Mountain View, CA 94043

IBM
1133 Westchester Ave.
White Plains, NY 10601

Nestar Systems
2585 Bayshore Road
Palo Alto, CA 94303

Norrell Data-Systems
1170 North Industrial Park
Orem, UT 84054

North Star Computers
1440 Catalina Street
San Leonardo, CA 94577

Ungerman-Bass
2650 Mission College Blvd.
Santa Clara, CA 25050

Xerox
1341 Bordeaux Drive
Sunnyvale, CA 94086

Phototypesetting Machine Manufacturers

Here's a list of companies selling phototypesetting machines. If you plan to publish a book, it'll be composed on one of these machines. Checking the Yellow Pages under *Typesetters* or contacting a manufacturer will lead you to a local phototypesetter who can arrange to set your book either from your disks or through telephone hookup.

A.M. Varityper
30 Vreeland Road
Florham Park, NJ 07936

Alphatype Corporation
7711 North Merimac Ave.
Niles, IL 60648

Harris Corporation
Composition Systems Division
PO Box 2080
Melbourne, FL 33290

Itex Graphic Products
35 Cellu Drive
Nashua, NH 03063

Merganthaller Linotype Company
201 Old Country Road
Melville, NY 11747

Wang Laboratories
One Industrial Avenue
Lowell, MA 01851

Computer Supplies

My name has turned up on a number of computer supply mailing lists. For those who would like to receive catalogs that list computer and word processor accessories (like ribbons, print wheels, paper, anti-static mats, glare reduction screens, cables, ergonomic furniture, etc.), I am including a list of the outfits sending me catalogs. Call any one of the companies listed to receive a virtual lifetime free subscription. Kidding aside, the catalogs are fun to browse through and will allow you to locate just about anything you might need for your system. They all have 800 numbers, so it won't even cost you a phone call to get your first catalogs.

ANSCO
800-421-1270

Borroughs
800-253-4083

Fidelity
800-328-3034

Global
800-645-1232

Moore
800-323-6230

NCR
800-543-4833

NEBS
800-225-9550

Priority One
800-423-5922

SJB Distributors
800-522-4893

Source Systems
800-323-9622

System Essentials
800-223-6694

Visible Products
800-323-0628

Try MacInker, a $50 system for reinking used ribbons when the WD-40 stops working. You get it from: Computer Friends, 100 Northwest 86th Ave., Portland, OR 97229.

Line Conditioning

These companies sell equipment to protect your computer from potential problems caused by variations in the power line:

Cuesta Systems Inc.
3440 Roberto Court
San Luis Obispo, CA 93401

Displex Inc.
79 Hazel Street
Cove, NY 11542

Dymarc Industries
7133 Rutherford Rd.
Baltimore, MD 21207

Electronic Specialists
171 South Main St.
Natick, MA 07160

Radio Shack
1800 One Tandy Center
Fort Worth, TX 76102

RKS Industries
4865 Scotts Valley Drive
Scotts Valley, CA 95066

Sun Research Inc.
Box 210
New Durham, NH 03855

Computer Repairs and Service

Here's hoping you never require the services of the companies on this list. However, each has nationwide computer and word processor service centers capable of repairing a wide variety of machines. If you're concerned about repairs and service, a maintenance contract can be purchased either from a company on the list or from the vendor that sold you the equipment, for a yearly cost of about 12 percent of your equipment's purchase price.

Bell & Howell
6800 McCormick Road
Chicago, IL 60645

Bunker Ramo Information Systems
35 Nutmeg Drive
Trumbull Industrial Park
Trumbull, CT 66609

Control Data Corp.
Engineering Services
5720 Smetana Drive
Minnetonka, MN 55343

Decision Data Computer Corp.
400 Horsham Road
Horsham, PA 19044

General Electronic Company
Instrumentation and Computer
  Service Department
One River Road
Schenectady, NY 12345

Indeserv
PO Box 92
531 King Street
Littleton, MA 01460

RCA Service Company
Route 30
Cherry Hill, NJ 08358

Sorbus Services
50 E. Swedesford Road
Trager, PA 19355

TRW
9841 Airport Blvd.
Los Angeles, CA 90045

Western Union Telegraph Co.
Field Services Division
7 Arrow Road
Upper Saddle River, NJ 07458

Information Utilities

For all you "infomaniacs," here's a list of information utilities to satisfy your most lustful cravings:

CompuServe
Information Services
500 Arlington Center
Columbus, Ohio 43220
$20-$40 to join;
$5-$22.50/hour

New York Times
Information Service
1719A, Route 10
Parsipanny, NJ 07054
$200 to join;
$65-$165/hour

Dialog
3460 Millview Ave.
Palo Alto, CA 94304
$165 to join;
$25-$500/hour

The SOURCE
1616 Anderson Road
McLean, VA 22102
$100 to join;
$5.75-$25.75/hour

Dow Jones News/Retrieval
PO Box 300
Princeton, NJ 08540
$50 to join;
$9-$72/hour

Computer Magazines

Business Computer Systems
Cahners Publishing Co.
221 Columbus Avenue
Boston, MA 02116

Computerworld
PO Box 880
375 Cochituate Road
Framingham, MA 01701

BYTE Magazine
70 Main Street
Peterborough, NH 03458

Creative Computing
39 East Hanover Ave.
Morris Plains, NJ 07950

Communications News
Harcourt Brace Jovanovich
125 First Street
Geneva, IL 60134

Data Communications
McGraw Hill
1221 Park Avenue
New York, NY 10020

Computer Business News
PO Box 880
375 Cochituate Road
Framingham, MA 01701

Desktop Computing
100100I Inc.
80 Pine Street
Peterborough, NH 03458

Computer Graphics World
Computer Graphics World
  Publishing Co.
1714 Stockton Street
San Francisco, CA 94133

80 Microcomputing
PO Box 981
Farmingdale, NY 11737

80-US Journal
3838 South Warner St.
Tacoma, WA 98409

*ICP Interface Administrative
& Accounting*
International Computer Programs
PO Box 40946
9000 Keystone Crossing
Indianapolis, IN 46240

Information & Records Management
PTN Publishing Corp.
101 Crossways Park West
Woodbury, NY 11797

Infosystems
Hitchcock Publishing Co.
Hitchcock Building
Wheaton, IL 60187

Infoworld
530 Lytton Ave.
Palo Alto, CA 94301

Journal of Systems Management
Association for Systems Management
24587 Bagley Road
Cleveland, OH 44138

Modern Office Procedures
Penton/IPC
Chester Avenue
Cleveland, OH 44114

Personal Computing
Hayden Publishing Co.
50 Essex Street
Rochelle Park, NJ 07662

PC Magazine
Ziff-Davis Publishing
One Park Ave.
New York, NY 10016

Popular Computing
70 Main Street
Peterborough, NH 03458

Sourceworld
Source Telecomputing Corp.
1616 Anderson Road
McLean, VA 22102

Word Processing & Information Systems
Geyer-McAlister Publications, Inc.
51-P Madison Avenue
New York, NY 10010

System Descriptions and Evaluations

Data Pro
1805 Underwood Blvd.
Delran, NJ 08075

Seybold Reports on Word Processing
PO Box 644
Media, PA 19063

Health Factors Resource List

Here's the most important section of this appendix. The people working in these organizations are some of the most devoted I have ever encountered. Try calling them, get copies of their reports, and offer them your support if it feels right.

American Newspaper Guild
AFL-CIO
1125 15th St. N.W.
Washington, DC 20005
(202) 296-2990
Publishes reports and conducts studies on VDT related health problems.

Committee on Vision
National Academy of Sciences
2101 Constitution Ave., N.W.
Washington, DC 20418
"Symposium on Vision and VDT Work"

National Institute for Occupational Safety and Health (NIOSH)
Parklawn Building
5600 Fishers Lane
Rockville, MD 20857
(301) 443-2140
Free detailed reports and studies of VDT related health problems. Report 81-129: *Potential Hazards of Video Display Terminals,* is a must.

N.Y. Committee on Safety and Health
32 Union Square
New York, NY 10003
Pamphlet: *Health Protection for Operators of VDT/CRT's*

Occupational Safety and Health Administration (OSHA)
U.S. Department of Labor
200 Constitution Ave., N.W.
Washington, DC 20210
(202) 523-8148

Office Hazards, by Joel Makir
Tilden Press
Washington, D.C.
Every office worker in America should read this book.

The VDT Manual
by Eakir, Hart and Stewart
Wiley and Sons
605 Third Ave.
New York, NY 10158
A great reference book.

Working Woman (9 to 5)
1224 Huron Rd.
Cleveland, OH 44115
Toll free: (800) 521-VDTS
Series of reports summarizing VDT and office problems.

Computer Insurance

If you use your computer for business, standard household policies may not cover your machine. A couple of alternatives are: Safeware (88 Broad St., Columbus, Ohio 43215), and the Association of Computer Users (P.O. Box 9003, Boulder, CO 80301). ACU not only provides coverage of the machine, but your program, text and data files as well.

APPENDIX IV: Public Access Bulletin Boards

All you need to use the following list of Public Access Bulletin Boards is a communications program that lets your machine function as a dumb terminal, and a modem. Most of the boards are run as a public service by either private individuals or computer businesses. Be prepared to spend a lot of time dialing and getting busy signals before getting through . . . most bulletin boards have a lot of users. The phone numbers followed by *24 are running 24 hours a day, so the wee hours of the morning are great times to connect. The letters -rb indicate systems that require you to dial the number, hang up after one ring and then call back. If you have a 1200 bps modem, run it at 300 bps on your first call, since all boards run 300 and only a small percentage run 300 and 1200.

When you finally get through, the system will ask you some questions about who you are and where you live. Don't get paranoid and start making up names and addresses. Treat the boards with integrity—their owners deserve it. Some of the boards may charge a subscription fee of $5 or $10 per year. Use your discretion on these, but remember that their owners are donating the use of their equipment and time. Look at the fee as a token of appreciation for the service.

Most systems will present a menu of options starting with instructions on how to work the system. Read these and then head for the electronic message center. Read some of the public messages. If your communications program has a *file transfer* or an *ASCII capture routine*, start downloading some programs or text or whatever to your machine. If your communications program cannot receive files, leave a public message that says something like this:

To: All
From: Fred Stern
Re: Communications Help Needed

I have a Qwerty computer with no communications software. I would like to get a copy of Modem 7 or any other file transfer program configured for my machine. Call 555-6421 or leave a message here.

                                                          Thank you.

You'll probably receive several calls offering free programs or suggestions on how to get started.

Most bulletin boards have the numbers of all other boards in the area. Use a number from the list to get started and to find out what other boards are around. Where did I get the list? I downloaded it from a local bulletin board. I ran it through my database program to sort it according to Area Codes, so you can locate the nearby bulletin boards quickly.

Have fun and welcome to the Computer Revolution!

Name	**Phone Number**
CBBS London, England . . . European Standard	1 399-2136
FORUM-80 Hull, England . . . , , , , , , ...	011 482-859169
ADBS Piscataway, NJ . . . Apple Group NJ	201 968-1074
ABBS Pompton Plains, NJ . . . CCNJ	201 835-7228

```
ABBS Saddlebrook, NJ ............................201 843-4563
A-C-C-E-S-S Wyckoff, NJ ........................201 891-7441*24
CONFERENCE-TREE Denville, NJ ..................201 627-5151*24
FORUM-80 Brielle, NJ . . . Monmouth ................201 528-6623*24
FORUM-80 Linden, NJ ............................201 486-2956*24
New Jersey TELECOM ............................201 635-0705*24
PHOTO-80 Haledon, NJ ...........................201 790-6795
PMS Piscataway, NJ . . . Rutgers U. Microlab ..........201 932-3887
PMS Shrewsbury, NJ .............................201 747-6768
RATS Little Falls, NJ .............................201 785-3565
RCP/M RBBS Ocean, NJ ..........................201 775-8705
RCP/M RBBS Piscataway, NJ . . . Rutgers U ............201 932-3879*24
RCP/M RIBBS Central, NJ ........................201 747-7301
RCP/M RIBBS Cranford, NJ . . . ACG-NJ .............201 272-1874*24
TAB Short Hills, NJ ...............................201 376-8055*24
ARMUDIC Washington, DC .........................202 276-8342
PSBBS Washington, DC . . . Program Store ............202 337-4694*24
                                                   202 960-2056*24
BULLET-80 Danbury, CT ..........................203 744-4644
MICRO-COM West Hartford, CT . . . Computer City ......203 227-1829
FORUM-80 Montgomery, AL ........................205 272-5069-rb
RCP/M RBBS Huntsville, AL ........................205 895-6749-rb
ABBS Seattle, WA . . . Apple Crate I ..................206 935-9119
ABBS Seattle, WA . . . Apple Crate II .................206 244-5438
A-C-C-E-S-S Olympia, WA ........................206 866-9043*24
AMIS Washington . . . S*P*A*C*E ..................206 226-1117
ARBB Seattle, WA ..............................206 546-6239
FORUM-80 Seattle, WA ..........................206 723-3282
JCTS Redmond, WA .............................206 883-0403*24
MAIL BOARD-82 Seattle, WA .....................206 527-0897*24
MINI-BIN Seattle, WA ...........................206 762-5141
MSG-80 Everett, WA ............................206 334-7394
PMS Bothell, WA . . . Software Unltd .................206 483-8101
RCP/M RBBS Yelm, WA ..........................206 458-3086-rb
SEACOMM-80 Seattle, WA .......................206 763-8879*24
ARMUDIC New York .............................212 598 0719
Brian Boyle's BBS Bronx, NY .....................212-933 9459
COMM-80 Queen's, NY ..........................212 897-3392*24
CONNECTION-80 Manhattan, NY ..................212 991-1664
CONNECTION-80 Woodhaven, NY ..................212 441-3755*24
PMS New York, NY . . . McGraw-Hill Books ...........212 997-2488
RCP/M AABB New York, NY . . . Astronomy ...........212 787-5520
SISTER Staten Island, NY .........................212-442 3874*24
SMBBS New York, NY ...........................212 884-5408
TCBBS New York, NY . . . B.A.M.S. .................212 362-1040*24
TCBBS New York, NY . . . Leigh's Comp Wrld .........212 879-7698*24
TCBBS New York, NY . . . W.E.B.B. ................212 799-4649
TFC New York, NY .............................212 799-9177*24
```

```
ABBS Los Angeles, CA . . . Pacific Palisades . . . . . . . . . . . 213 459-6400
ABBS Santa Monica, CA . . . Computer Conspiracy . . . . . . . 213 829-1140
BBS Los Angeles, CA . . . B.R. . . . . . . . . . . . . . . . . . . . 213 394-5950*24
CONFERENCE-TREE . . . 1 Santa Monica, CA . . . . . . . . . 213 394-1525*24
CONFERENCE-TREE . . . #71 Beverly Hills, CA . . . . . . . 213 372-4800
HBBS San Fernando Valley . . . . . . . . . . . . . . . . . . . . . . . 213 366-4837
Kluge Computer Whittier, CA . . . . . . . . . . . . . . . . . . . . . 213 947-8128*24
L.A. Interchange Los Angeles, CA . . . . . . . . . . . . . . . . . . 213 631-3186*24
NET-WORKS Encino, CA . . . . . . . . . . . . . . . . . . . . . . . . 213 345-3670
NET-WORKS Los Angeles, CA . . . Coin Games . . . . . . . . 213 336-5535
NET-WORKS Los Angeles, CA . . . Computer World . . . . . 213 859-0894*24
NET-WORKS Los Angeles, CA . . . Mag. Fantasies . . . . . . 213 388-5198
NET-WORKS Pirate's Inn . . . . . . . . . . . . . . . . . . . . . . . . 213 454-3075
Novation Co. Los Angeles, CA . . . (pass=CAT) . . . . . . . . 213 881-6880-rb
PASBBS Bellflower, CA . . . . . . . . . . . . . . . . . . . . . . . . . 213 531-1057
PASBBS Torrance, CA . . . . . . . . . . . . . . . . . . . . . . . . . . 213 516-7089*24
PMS Los Angeles, CA . . . . . . . . . . . . . . . . . . . . . . . . . . 213 334-7614*24
PMS Woodland Hills, CA . . . O.A.C. . . . . . . . . . . . . . . . . 213 346-1849*24
RCP/M CBBS Pasadena, CA . . . . . . . . . . . . . . . . . . . . . 213 799-1632*24
RCP/M RBBS Los Angeles, CA . . . Granada Engr . . . . . . . 213 360-5053
RCP/M RBBS Palos Verdes, CA . . . GFRN Data Xch . . . . 213 541-2503*24
DRAGON'S GAME SYSTEM . . . (pass=DRAGON) . . . . . 213 428-5206
LONG BEACH COMMUNITY COMPUTER . . . . . . . . . . 213 591-7239*24
ABBS Dallas, TX . . . Dallas Info Board . . . . . . . . . . . . . . 214 248-4539
ABBS Dallas, TX . . . The Moon . . . . . . . . . . . . . . . . . . . . 214 931-3437*24
BBS-80 Dallas, TX . . . DALTRUG . . . . . . . . . . . . . . . . . . 214 235-8784*24
BULLET-80 Hawkins, TX . . . . . . . . . . . . . . . . . . . . . . . . 214 769-3036*24
BULLET-80 Tyler, TX . . . . . . . . . . . . . . . . . . . . . . . . . . . 214 595-4217
NET-WORKS Dallas, TX . . . . . . . . . . . . . . . . . . . . . . . . 214 361-1386*24
NET-WORKS Dallas, TX . . . Apple Shack . . . . . . . . . . . . 214 644-4781*24
NET-WORKS Dallas, TX . . . Winesap . . . . . . . . . . . . . . . 214 824-7455
BULLET-80 Langhorne, PA . . . . . . . . . . . . . . . . . . . . . . 215 364-2180
HERMES-80 Allentown, PA . . . . . . . . . . . . . . . . . . . . . . 215 434-3998
Lehigh Press BB, PA . . . . . . . . . . . . . . . . . . . . . . . . . . . 215 435-3388
RCP/M RBBS Allentown, PA . . . . . . . . . . . . . . . . . . . . . 215 398-3937*24
ABBS Akron, OH . . . Akron Digital Group . . . . . . . . . . . . 216 745-7855*24
ABBS Cleveland, OH . . . . . . . . . . . . . . . . . . . . . . . . . . . 216 779-1338
ARMUDIC Ohio . . . . . . . . . . . . . . . . . . . . . . . . . . . . . . 216 582-2797
BULLET-80 Akron, OH . . . . . . . . . . . . . . . . . . . . . . . . . 216 645-0827*24
BULLET-80 Chesterland, OH . . . . . . . . . . . . . . . . . . . . . 216 729-2769
FORUM-80 Cleveland, OH . . . . . . . . . . . . . . . . . . . . . . . 216 486-4176
PMS Akron, OH . . . RAUG . . . . . . . . . . . . . . . . . . . . . . 216 867-7463*24
PMS Massillon, OH . . . . . . . . . . . . . . . . . . . . . . . . . . . . 216 832-8392*24
BULLET-80 Springfield, IL . . . . . . . . . . . . . . . . . . . . . . 217 529-1113
NET-WORKS Decatur, IL . . . C.A.M.S. . . . . . . . . . . . . . . 217 429-5541
A-C-C-E-S-S Annapolis, MD . . . . . . . . . . . . . . . . . . . . . 301 267-7666*24
AMIS Rockville, MD . . . Pirate's Cove . . . . . . . . . . . . . . 301 881-3007*24
ARMUDIC Silver Spring, MD . . . Computer Age . . . . . . . 301 587-2132*24
```

```
CBBS Gaithersburg, MD . . . CPEUG . . . . . . . . . . . . . . . . . 301 948-5717*24
CONNECTION -80 Gaithersburg, MD . . . . . . . . . . . . . . . . 301 840-8588*24
HEX Silver Spring, MD . . . . . . . . . . . . . . . . . . . . . . . . . . . 301 593-7033*24
IBMPC BBS Gaithersburg, MD . . . . . . . . . . . . . . . . . . . . . 301 948-8877*24
IBMPC BBS Gaithersburg, MD . . . (Pwd=IBMPC) . . . . . . 301 251-6293*24
IBMPC BBS Rockville, MD . . . (Pwd=IBMPC) . . . . . . . . . 301 949-8848*24
Laurel BBS Laurel, MD . . . . . . . . . . . . . . . . . . . . . . . . . . . . 301 953-3753
PMS Ellicott City, MD . . . . . . . . . . . . . . . . . . . . . . . . . . . . 301 465-3176
PMS Pikesville, MD . . . . . . . . . . . . . . . . . . . . . . . . . . . . . 301 653-3413
RCP/M HYDRA Gaithersburg, MD . . . MicroLab . . . . . . . 301 948-5718*24
Remote Northstar NASA, Greenbelt, MD . . . . . . . . . . . . . . 301 344-9156
Remote Northstar Silver Spring, MD . . . . . . . . . . . . . . . . . 301 593-3042
ABBS Denver, CO . . . . . . . . . . . . . . . . . . . . . . . . . . . . . . . 303 759-2625
CONNECTION-80 Denver, CO . . . . . . . . . . . . . . . . . . . . . 303 690-4566*24
CoxCo Arvada, CO . . . . . . . . . . . . . . . . . . . . . . . . . . . . . . 303 423-5001*24
FORUM-80 Denver, CO . . . . . . . . . . . . . . . . . . . . . . . . . . 303 341-0636*24
FORUM-80 Denver, CO . . . #2 . . . . . . . . . . . . . . . . . . . . . 303 399-8858
RCP/M RBBS Colorado Springs, CO . . . Arvada Elect . . . . 303 634-1158*24
TARIBOARD Ft. Collins, CO . . . . . . . . . . . . . . . . . . . . . . . 303 221-1779
UFONET Golden, CO . . . Sci Fi . . . . . . . . . . . . . . . . . . . . . 303 278 4244*24
ABBS Ft. Lauderdale, FL . . . Byte Shop . . . . . . . . . . . . . . . 305 486-2983
ABBS Miami, FL . . . Byte Shop . . . . . . . . . . . . . . . . . . . . . 305 261-3600
ABBS West Palm Beach, FL . . . . . . . . . . . . . . . . . . . . . . . . 305 848-3802
AMIS Miami, FL . . . APOGEE . . . . . . . . . . . . . . . . . . . . . 305 238-1231-rb
BBS Homestead, FL . . . . . . . . . . . . . . . . . . . . . . . . . . . . . . 305 246-1111
CONNECTION-80 Orlando, FL . . . . . . . . . . . . . . . . . . . . . 305 644-8327*24
CONNECTION-80 Winter Garden, FL . . . . . . . . . . . . . . . . 305 877-2829*24
FORUM-80 Ft. Lauderdale, FL . . . . . . . . . . . . . . . . . . . . . 305 772-4444*24
Joke BBS Pompano Beach, FL . . . . . . . . . . . . . . . . . . . . . . 305 974-0040
MICRO-80 West Palm Beach, FL . . . . . . . . . . . . . . . . . . . 305 686-3695
MOUSE-NET Orlando, FL . . . . . . . . . . . . . . . . . . . . . . . . . 305 277-0473*24
NET-WORKS Miami, FL . . . Big Apple . . . . . . . . . . . . . . . 305 948-8000
PMS-80 Deerfield Beach, FL . . . . . . . . . . . . . . . . . . . . . . . 305 427-6300*24
RCP/M RBBS South Florida . . . . . . . . . . . . . . . . . . . . . . . 305 255-6027
TRADE-80 Ft. Lauderdale, FL . . . . . . . . . . . . . . . . . . . . . . 305 525-1192
ABBS Peoria, IL . . . . . . . . . . . . . . . . . . . . . . . . . . . . . . . . . 309 692-6502
ABBS Chicago, IL . . . Gamemaster . . . . . . . . . . . . . . . . . . 312 475-4884*24
ABBS Chicago, IL . . . Rogers Park . . . . . . . . . . . . . . . . . . . 312 973-2227
ABBS Downers Grove, IL . . . . . . . . . . . . . . . . . . . . . . . . . . 312 964-7768
ABBS Glen Ellyn, IL . . . CODE . . . . . . . .  . . . . . . . . . . . . 312 537-7063*24
ABBS Naperville, IL . . . Illini Microcomputer . . . . . . . . . . 312 420-7995
ABBS Oak Brook IL . . . AIMS . . . . . . . . . . . . . . . . . . . . . . 312 789-0499*24
ABBS Oak Brook, IL . . . Oak Brook Computer . . . . . . . . . 312 941-9009
BBS Chicago, IL . . . Electronic Exchange . . . . . . . . . . . . . 312 541-6470*24
CBBS Chicago, IL . . . . . . . . . . . . . . . . . . . . . . . . . . . . . . . . 312 545-8086*24
FBBS Skokie, IL . . . . . . . . . . . . . . . . . . . . . . . . . . . . . . . . . 312 677-8514
MARS/RP Rogers Park, IL . . . . . . . . . . . . . . . . . . . . . . . . . 312 743-8176*24
MCMS Chicago, IL . . . C.A.M.S. . . . . . . . . . . . . . . . . . . . . 312 927-1020*24
```

```
MCMS Chicago, IL . . . MESSAGE-82 . . . . . . . . . . . . . . . . . 312 622-4442*24
MCMS Round Lake, IL . . . A.M.S. . . . . . . . . . . . . . . . . . . 312 740-9128*24
MCMS Schaumburg, IL . . . WACO Hot Line . . . (pvt) . . . . 312 351-4374*24
MCMS Wheaton, IL . . . Metro West Database . . . . . . . . . . 312 260-0640*24
NESSY Chicago, IL . . . . . . . . . . . . . . . . . . . . . . . . . . . . . . 312 773-3308
NESSY Palatine, IL . . . Terry and Gwen's . . . . . . . . . . . . . 312 289-6393
NET-WORKS Arlington Heights, IL . . . CLAH . . . . . . . . . 312 255-6489
NET-WORKS Chicago, IL . . . Pirate's Ship . . . . . . . . . . . . . 312 935-2933*24
NET-WORKS Lake Forest, IL . . . V-N-A . . . . . . . . . . . . . 312 295-7284
NET-WORKS II Chicago, IL . . . Chipmunk . . . . . . . . . . . . . 312 323-3741*24
PBBS Palatine, IL . . . Co-operative Comp Svc . . . . . . . . . . 312 359-9450*24
PMS Arlington Heights, IL . . . . . . . . . . . . . . . . . . . . . . . . 312 870-7176*24
PMS Chicago, IL . . . . . . . . . . . . . . . . . . . . . . . . . . . . . . . 312 373-8057*24
PMS Lake Forest, IL . . . NIAUG . . . . . . . . . . . . . . . . . . . . 312 295-6926*24
RATS Homewood, IL . . . CMMS . . . . . . . . . . . . . . . . . . . . 312 957-3924
RCP/M CBBS Chicago, IL . . . HUG . . . . . . . . . . . . . . . . . . 312 671-4992*24
RCP/M CBBS Lake Forest, IL . . . CCCC . . . . . . . . . . . . . . 312 234-9257
RCP/M Chicago, IL . . . Logan Square . . . . . . . . . . . . . . . . 312 252-2136
RCP/M Palatine, IL . . . . . . . . . . . . . . . . . . . . . . . . . . . . . 312 359-2553-rb
RCP/M RBBS Hyde Park, IL . . . . . . . . . . . . . . . . . . . . . . 312 955-4493
RCP/M TRS-80 Chicago, IL . . . . . . . . . . . . . . . . . . . . . . . 312 949-6189
ABBS Detroit, MI . . . . . . . . . . . . . . . . . . . . . . . . . . . . . . . 313 477-4471
ABBS Southfield, MI . . . Michigan Info-Fone . . . . . . . . . . 313 357-1422
AMIS Detroit, MI . . . M.A.C.E. . . . . . . . . . . . . . . . . . . . . 313 868-2064*24
AMIS Sterling Hts, MI . . . ARCADE . . . . . . . . . . . . . . . . 313 978-8087*24
BULLET-80 Mt. Clemens, MI . . . Medical . . . . . . . . . . . . 313 465-9531-rb
FORUM-80 Pontiac, MI . . . . . . . . . . . . . . . . . . . . . . . . . . 313 335-8456
RCP/M Detroit, MI . . . . . . . . . . . . . . . . . . . . . . . . . . . . . 313 584-1044-rb
RCP/M MCBBS Detroit, MI . . . (pass=Sorcerer) . . . . . . . 313 535-9186-rb
RCP/M MCBBS Royal Oak, MI . . . Keith Petersen . . . . . . 313 759-6569-rb
RCP/M MCBBS TCBBS Dearborn, MI . . . . . . . . . . . . . . . 313 846-6127*24
RCP/M RBBS Southfield, MI . . . . . . . . . . . . . . . . . . . . . . 313 559-5326*24
RCP/M RBBS Westland, MI . . . . . . . . . . . . . . . . . . . . . . . 313 729-1905-rb
TREND-NET Detroit, MI . . . . . . . . . . . . . . . . . . . . . . . . . 313 775-1649
Westside Download Detroit, MI . . . . . . . . . . . . . . . . . . . . 313 533-0254
Bunkie's Place . . . . . . . . . . . . . . . . . . . . . . . . . . . . . . . . . 313 683-5076
Davy Jones Locker . . . . . . . . . . . . . . . . . . . . . . . . . . . . . . 313 764-1837*24-r
Legend Industries BBS . . . . . . . . . . . . . . . . . . . . . . . . . . . 313 674-1849
Michigan Apple-Fone . . . . . . . . . . . . . . . . . . . . . . . . . . . 313 295-0783
Twilight Phone . . . . . . . . . . . . . . . . . . . . . . . . . . . . . . . . . 313 775-1649
ABBS St. Louis, MO . . . . . . . . . . . . . . . . . . . . . . . . . . . . 314 838-7784*24
ABBS St. Louis, MO . . . Century Next Computers . . . . . . 314 442-6502
NET-WORKS St. Louis, MO . . . Computer Station . . . . . . 314 432-7120
NET-WORKS II St. Louis, MO . . . Advance Data . . . . . . . 314 781-1308
SLAMS St. Louis, MO . . . . . . . . . . . . . . . . . . . . . . . . . . . 314 839-4307
FORUM-80 Wichita, KA . . . . . . . . . . . . . . . . . . . . . . . . . . 316 682-2113*24
PMS Indianapolis, IN . . . . . . . . . . . . . . . . . . . . . . . . . . . . 317 787-5486*24
FORUM-80 Shreveport, LA . . . . . . . . . . . . . . . . . . . . . . . 318 631-7107*24
```

```
ABBS Iowa City, IA . . . Apple-Med . . . . . . . . . . . . . . . . . . 319 353-6528
CBBS Cedar Rapids, IA  . . . . . . . . . . . . . . . . . . . . . . . . . 319 364-0811
NET-WORKS Providence, RI . . . Computer City . . . . . . . . 401 331-8450*24
ABBS Lincoln, NE  . . . . . . . . . . . . . . . . . . . . . . . . . . . . . 402 423-8086*24
ABBS Omaha, NE . . . . . . . . . . . . . . . . . . . . . . . . . . . . . . 402 339-7809
TRADE-80 Omaha, NE . . . . . . . . . . . . . . . . . . . . . . . . . . 402 292-6184
RCP/M RBBS Edmonton, Alberta, Canada . . . Computron . 403 454-6093*24
ABBS Atlanta, GA . . . AGS  . . . . . . . . . . . . . . . . . . . . . . . 404 733-3461*24
ABBS Atlanta, GA . . . #X  . . . . . . . . . . . . . . . . . . . . . . . . 404 256-1549
ABBS Augusta, GA . . . Bailey's Computer Store . . . . . . . . 404 790-8614
ATABBS Atlanta, GA . . . . . . . . . . . . . . . . . . . . . . . . . . . . 404 252-9438*24
ATABBS Georgia  . . . . . . . . . . . . . . . . . . . . . . . . . . . . . . 404 434-1168-rb
BULLET-80 Fayetteville, GA . . . . . . . . . . . . . . . . . . . . . . 404 461-9686
CBBS Atlanta, GA . . . . . . . . . . . . . . . . . . . . . . . . . . . . . . 404 394-4220*24
IBMPC BBS Atlanta, GA  . . . . . . . . . . . . . . . . . . . . . . . . 404 252-9438*24
ITBBS Atlanta, GA  . . . . . . . . . . . . . . . . . . . . . . . . . . . . . 404 498-2392
MBBS Atlanta, GA  . . . . . . . . . . . . . . . . . . . . . . . . . . . . . 404 894-7765*24
Remote Northstar Atlanta, GA . . . . . . . . . . . . . . . . . . . . . 404 926-4318*24
SCANBOARD-80 Atlanta, GA . . . . . . . . . . . . . . . . . . . . . 404 457-8384
TELEMESSAGE-80 Atlanta, GA . . . . . . . . . . . . . . . . . . . 404 962-0616
ARMUDIC Oklahoma City, OK . . . Grekelcom . . . . . . . . . 405 722-5056*24
IBMPC BBS Billings, MT . . . . . . . . . . . . . . . . . . . . . . . . 406 656-9624
ABBS Campbell, CA . . . PCnet . . . . . . . . . . . . . . . . . . . . 408 378-3713
AMIS California . . . IBBBS . . . . . . . . . . . . . . . . . . . . . . . 408 298-6930
AMIS Cupertino, CA . . . Grafex Co . . . . . . . . . . . . . . . . . 408 253-5216
AMIS San Jose, CA . . . CIOBBS  . . . . . . . . . . . . . . . . . . . 408 244-6229*24
BBS Sunnyvale, CA . . . . . . . . . . . . . . . . . . . . . . . . . . . . . 408 735-8181
BULLET-80 San Jose, CA . . . . . . . . . . . . . . . . . . . . . . . . 408 241-0769
CBBS Sunnyvale, CA  . . . . . . . . . . . . . . . . . . . . . . . . . . . 408 737-7543
Compunet Santa Clara, CA  . . . . . . . . . . . . . . . . . . . . . . 408 727-8060
CONNECTION-80 San Jose, CA  . . . . . . . . . . . . . . . . . . 408 997-2790
LBBS San Jose, CA  . . . . . . . . . . . . . . . . . . . . . . . . . . . . 408 997-6148
NET-WORKS San Jose, CA . . . Comp-at-Law . . . . . . . . . . 408 265-8070
NET-WORKS San Jose, CA . . . Computer Emporium . . . . . 408 227-5416
Oxgate Milpitas, CA  . . . . . . . . . . . . . . . . . . . . . . . . . . . 408 263-2588-rb
Oxgate San Jose, CA  . . . . . . . . . . . . . . . . . . . . . . . . . . . 408 287-5901
PMS Campbell, CA . . . Databank  . . . . . . . . . . . . . . . . . . 408 370-0873*24
PMS Santa Clara, CA  . . . . . . . . . . . . . . . . . . . . . . . . . . 408 554-9036
PMS Santa Cruz, Aptos, CA . . . . . . . . . . . . . . . . . . . . . . 408 688-9629*24
                                                             408 429-1995
RCP/M Santa Clara, CA  . . . . . . . . . . . . . . . . . . . . . . . . 408 246-5014*24
AMIS Pittsburgh, PA . . . P.A.C.E. . . . . . . . . . . . . . . . . . . 412 655-2652
CBBS Pittsburgh, PA . . . PACC . . . . . . . . . . . . . . . . . . . . 412 822-7176*24
Western Massachusetts Computer Club . . . . . . . . . . . . . . . 413 733-1749*24
ABBS Racine, WI . . . Colortron Computer . . . . . . . . . . . . 414 637-9990*24
BIGTOP Milwaukee, WI . . . . . . . . . . . . . . . . . . . . . . . . . 414 259-9475
Pet BBS Milwaukee, WI  . . . . . . . . . . . . . . . . . . . . . . . . 414 282-8118
Pet BBS Racine, WI . . . SEWPUG  . . . . . . . . . . . . . . . . . 414 554-9520*24
```

```
RCP/M Milwaukee, WI ... Rick Martinek .............. 414 774-2683-rb
RCP/M Milwaukee, WI ... MAUDE ................ 414 241-8364*24
ABBS Fremont, CA ... Computerland ................ 415 794-9214
ABBS Fremont, CA ... Zoram Assoc ................ 415 792-8406
ABBS Hayward, CA ... Byte Shop ................... 415 881-5662
ABBS Mill Valley, CA ........................... 415 383-0473
ABBS San Francisco, CA ... PCnet ................. 415 863-4703*24
CBBS San Leandro, CA ... Proxima ................. 415 357-1130
CONNECTION-80 Fremont, CA .................... 415 651-4147*24
CONNECTION-80 Hayward, CA .................... 415 278-6541
CONFERENCE-TREE #2 San Francisco, CA ........... 415 928-0641
CONFERENCE-TREE #4 Hayward, CA ... Forth IG .... 415 538-3580*24
CONFERENCE-TREE Berkeley, CA ................. 415 475-7101
CONFERENCE-TREE Berkeley, CA ... MicroWorks .... 415 548-4683
CONFERENCE-TREE San Francisco, CA ............. 415 552-2890
CONFERENCE-TREE Pacifica, CA ................. 415 359-5708
Download-80 Concord, CA ........................ 415 827-5549
FORUM-80 San Francisco, CA ..................... 415 348-2139
IAC Message Base Menlo Park, CA .................. 415 367-1339*24
INFO-NET Foster City, CA ........................ 415 349-3126
INFO-System San Leandro, CA .................... 415 895-8980
LBBS Menlo Park, CA ... Living Videotext ............ 415 327-8876*24
LBBS San Francisco, CA ......................... 415 863-7715
NET-WORKS San Francisco, CA ... Apple Core ........ 415 585-6334
NET-WORKS San Francisco, CA ... SFACBS ......... 415 239-0312
PMS Palo Alto, CA .............................. 415 493-7691*24
PMS Pleasanton, CA ............................ 415 462-7419*24
PMS Portola Valley, CA .......................... 415 851-3453*24
RCP/M RBBS Belmont, CA ... Datanet .............. 415 595-0541
RCP/M RBBS Larkspur, CA ....................... 415 461-7726*24
TAB San Rafael, CA ... Adventure ................. 415 457-4467
RCP/M Mississauga, Ontario, Canada ............... 416 826-5394*24
ABBS Toledo, OH ... ABACUS II ................... 419 865-1594
ABBS Toledo, OH ... Computer Store ............... 419 531-3845
CONNECTION-80 Little Rock, AR .................. 501 372-0576
ABBS Louisville, KY ............................ 502 245-7811*24
ABBS Portland, OR ............................. 503 641-8555*24
ARMUDIC Eugene, OR ... ACE .................... 503 343-4352
CBBS Portland, OR ... NW ...................... 503 646-5510*24
CONNECTION-80 Portland, OR ... PAUG ............ 503 928-0301*24
FORUM-80 Medford, OR ......................... 503 535-6883*24
ABBS Baton Rouge, LA .......................... 504 291-1360
CBBS Baton Rouge, LA .......................... 504 273-3116*24
NET-WORKS Baton Rouge, LA ... Crescent City ....... 504 454-6688
ABBS Spokane, WA ............................. 509 456-8900
ABBS Spokane, WA ... Electro-Mart ............... 509 534-2419*24
ATARI BBS Ash, WA ............................. 509 575-7704
A2-D2 Kennewick, WA ... Kennewick Comp Co ........ 509 582-5217
```

```
PMS Richland, WA ............................... 509 943-6502*24
ABBS San Antonio, TX ............................ 512 737-0214*24
CBBS Corpus Christi, TX ........................... 512 855-1512
CONFERENCE-TREE #22 Victoria, TX .............. 512 578-5833
FORUM-80 San Antonio, TX ....................... 512 340-6720
NET-WORKS Corpus Christi, TX ... Sparklin' City ...... 512 882-6569
ORACLE Classified System Austin, TX ................ 512 346-4495
BBS-80 Cincinnati, OH ............................ 513 244-2983
PMS Cincinnati, OH .............................. 513 671-2753
XBBS Hamilton, OH ............................... 513 863-7681*24
NET-WORKS Montreal, Canada ..................... 514 937-2188*24
ABBS Ames, IA ................................... 515 294-8204
NET-WORKS Des Moines, IA ... Computer Emporium ... 515 279-8863
ABBS Long Island, NY ... Pirates Cove ............... 516 698-4008
CBBS Long Island, NY ............................. 516 334-3134*24
CBBS Long Island, NY ... LICA LIMBS .............. 516 561-6590*24
CONNECTION-80 Centereach, NY ................... 516 588-5836
CONNECTION-80 Great Neck, NY .................. 516 482-8491*24
RCP/M RBBS Long Island, NY ...................... 516 698-8619-rb
RCP/M RBBS New York, NY ....................... 516 791-1767
ADVENTURE BBS ............................... 516 621-9296
CONNECTION-80 Lansing, MI ...................... 517 339-3367
Capital City BBS Albany, NY ....................... 518 346-3596*24
FORUM-80 Albany, NY ............................ 518 785-8478
Remote Apple Jackson, MS ......................... 601 992-1918*24-rb
ABBS Phoenix, AZ ............................... 602 898-0891
A-C-C-E-S-S Phoenix, AZ .......................... 602 996-9709*24
A-C-C-E-S-S Phoenix, AZ .......................... 602 957-4428*24
A-C-C-E-S-S Phoenix, AZ .......................... 602 274-5964
A-C-C-E-S-S Scottsdale, AZ ......................... 602 998-9411*24
CBBS Tucson, AZ ... TSG .......................... 602 746-3956*24
ABBS Nashua, NH ... Vibbs ........................ 603 888-6648
CONNECTION-80 Peterborough, NH ................ 603 924-7920
FORUM-80 Nashua, NH ........................... 603 882-5041
NET-WORKS Portsmouth, NH .. .................... 603 436-3461
ABBS Vancouver, B.C., Canada .................... 604 437-7001
CBBS Prince George, B.C., Canada .................. 604 562-9515
CBBS Vancouver, B.C., Canada .................... 604 687-2640*24
RCP/M Vancouver, B.C., Canada .................. 604 584-2543
RCP/M SJBBS Johnson City, NY .................... 607 797-6416
AMIS Madison, WI ... Magic Lantern ................ 608 251-8538
ABBS Turnersville, NJ ............................ 609 228-1149
RATS Oak Valley, NJ ............................. 609 468-5293
RATS Pittman, NJ ................................ 609 589-9241*24
RATS Wenonah, NJ ............................... 609 468-3844*24
THY BBS New Jersey .............................. 609 896-2436
CBBS Richfield, MN .............................. 612 869-5780
MCMS Minneapolis, MN ... NC Software ............ 612 533-1957*24
```

```
PMS Minneapolis, MN  ............................. 612 929-6699*24
ABBS Ottawa, Ontario, Canada . . . Compumart  ......... 613 725-2243
BULLETT-80 Ironton, OH  ......................... 614 532-6920
RCP/M CBBS Columbus, OH ...................... 614 272-2227*24
ABBS Kalamazoo, MI . . . Computer Room  ............ 616 382-0101
AMIS Grand Rapids, MI . . . GRASS  ................. 616 241-1971*24
CONNECTION-80 W. Mich . . . Micro Group, MI  ....... 616 457-1840*24
AMIS Boston, MA . . . Starbase 12  ................... 617 876-4885
CBBS Boston, MA ................................. 617 646-3610*24
CBBS Boston, MA . . . Lawrence General Hospital  ....... 617 683-2119
FORUM-80 Westford, MA  ......................... 617 692-3973
NET-WORKS Boston, MA . . . Pirate's Harbor  ......... 617 494-1985
New England Comp. Soc . . . Maynard, MA  ............. 617 897-0346
PMS Danvers, MA . . . Computer City  ................ 617 774-7516
PMS Weymouth, MA . . . Apple Guild  ................ 617 767-1303*24
RCP/M MCBBS Lexington, MA . . . Superbrain  ......... 617 862-0781
NET-WORKS Granite City, IL  ...................... 618 877-2904
NET-WORKS St. Louis, MO . . . Warlock's Castle  ....... 618 345-6638
NET-WORKS Grand Fork, ND . . . Armadillo  ........... 701 746-4959
ABBS Las Vegas, NV . . . Apple Cider  ................ 702 454-3417
FORUM-80 Las Vegas, NV ......................... 702 362-3609*24
SIGNON Reno, NV . . . (pswd=FREE) ................. 702 826-7234
ABBS Washington, DC  ........................... 703 560-7803*24
ABBS Washington, DC . . . Software Sorcery  ........... 703 255-2192
CHUG Bulletin Board Fairfax, VA  ................... 703 360-3812*24
CARRIER 2 Alexandria, VA ......................... 703 823-5210
CBBS Washington, DC . . . AMRAD  ................. 703 734-1387*24
FORUM-80 Fairfax, VA . . . Family Historians  ......... 703 978-7561
FORUM-80 Prince William County, VA  .............. 703 670-5881*24
IBM PCUG Annandale, VA  ........................ 703 560-0979*24
Potomac Micro Magic Inc., Falls Church, VA  .......... 703 379-0303*24
Switchboard Alexandria, VA ........................ 703 765-2161*24
TCUC BBS Springfield, VA  ........................ 703 451-8475
TCUG BBS Washington, DC  ....................... 703 960-2056*24
TRSBBS Annandale, VA ........................... 703 978-9754
CONFERENCE-TREE #84 Sonoma County, CA  ........ 707 996-2427*24
TRADE-80 Holstein, IA  ........................... 712 368-2656
TRADE-80 Sioux City, IA . . . Byte Exchange  .......... 712 274-2348
ABBS College Station, TX . . . Young's Elect Svc  ....... 713 693-3462*24
ABBS Houston, TX . . . Madam Bokeatha Society  ........ 713 455-9502
BULLET-80 Houston, TX  .......................... 713 331-2599
*PMS Freeport, TX . . . Gulfcoast  .................. 713 233-7943*24
BULLET-80 Anaheim, CA . . . Orange County  ........... 714 952-2110
BULLET-80 Riverside, CA  ......................... 714 359-3189
DIMENSION-80 Orange, CA  ....................... 714 974-9788
FORUM-80 Anaheim, CA . . . Orange County  ........... 714 545-9549
NET-WORKS Costa Mesa, CA . . . Info Net  ............ 714 545-7359
OCTUG BBS Fullerton, CA  ........................ 714 530-8226
```

```
ONLINE Santee, CA ... (ID=GUEST, pswd=PASS) .... 714 561-7271*24
Orange County Data Exchange Garden Grove, CA ........ 714 537-7913
PMS Anaheim, CA ... **IF** ...................... 714 772-8868*24
PMS Escondido, CA .............................. 714 746-0667
PMS San Diego, CA .............................. 714 582-9557*24
PMS Santee, CA ................................. 714 561-7277*24
RCP/M RBBS Anaheim, CA ... ANAHUG ............. 714 774-7860*24
RCP/M RBBS Garden Grove, CA ... GFRN Data Xch .... 714 534-1547*24
RCP/M RBBS San Diego, CA ....................... 714 271-5615
North Orange County Computer Club ................. 714 633-5240
CBBS Rochester, NY ... RAMS ..................... 716 244-9531
RCP/M RBS Rochester, NY ........................ 716 223-1100*24
BULLET-80 Clarks Summit, PA ..................... 717 586-2112
ABBS Essex Junction, VT .......................... 802 879-4981*24
CONFERENCE-TREE #38 Stowe, VT ................ 802 253-9377
ST80-CC Burlington, VT ... Lance Micklus, Inc ......... 802 862-7023*24
Compusystems Columbia, SC ....................... 803 771-0922
FORUM-80 Augusta, GA ........................... 803 279-5392-rb
FORUM-80 Charleston, SC ........................ 803 552-1612*24
Remote Northstar Virginia Beach, VA ................. 804 340-5246
TALK-80 Portsmouth, VA ... ROBB ................. 804 484-9636
BULLET-80 Lancaster,CA ......................... 805 947-9925
Computer Arts Message System Newhall, CA .......... 805 255-6445
RCP/M CBBS Simi Valley, CA ... CP/M Net ........... 805 527-9321
RCP/M RBBS Thousand Oaks, CA ................. 805 496-9522*24
Remote Northstar Santa Barbara, CA ................. 805 682-7876
ABBS Amarillo, TX ... Computer Corner ........... 806 355-5610
BULLET-80 Littlefield, TX ......................... 806 385-6843
ATARI BBS Hawaii ............................... 808 833-2616
NET-WORKS Hawaii ............................. 808 521-7312
CBBS Bloomington, IN ........................... 812 334-2522
ALPHA Tampa, FL ... (acct=ABCDOO, pwd=TRYIT) .. 813 251-4095*24
OMEGA Tampa, FL .............................. 813 257-2705*24
CONNECTION-80 Tampa, FL ...................... 813 977-0989
FORUM-80 Tampa, FL ... Wild Goose Board .......... 813 988-7400*24
RCP/M Tampa, FL .............................. 813 831-7276
Remote Northstar Largo, FL ....................... 813 535-9341*24
ST80-CC Tampa, FL ... Buddy's Super BB ............ 813 885-6187
ST80-CC Tampa, FL ... EAPBB General Store ......... 813 986-3128
BRADLEY Computer BBS ........................ 813 734-7103
COMPUTERIZED MESSAGE SYSTEM .............. 813 238-0299
H.A.M.S. ...................................... 813 986-6433*24
MICRO INFORMER ............................. 813 884-1506
TRADE-80 Erie, PA ............................. 814 898-2952*24
MCMS Lockport, IL ... J.A.M.S. .................... 815 828-1020*24
FORUM-80 Kansas City, MO ...................... 816 861-7040*24
FORUM-80 Kansas City, MO ... Market-80 ........... 816 931-9316
CBBS Waco, TX ................................ 817 776-1375
```

```
FORUM-80 Wichita Falls, TX  ......................817 855-3916
NET-WORKS Ft. Worth, TX...Computer Pro ..........817 732-1787
ABBS Memphis, TN  ..............................901 725-5691
ABBS Memphis, TN...Computer Lab  ...............901 761-4743
FORUM-80 Memphis, TN...Medical .................901 276-8196*24
ABBS Destin, FL...Ft. Walton Beach  .............904 243-1257
BBS Pensacola, FL  ..............................904 477-8783
ABBS Ketchikan, AK  .............................907 225-6789
CONFERNECE-TREE Anchorage, AK  ...............907 344-5251
PMS Anchorage, AK  ..............................907 344-8558
EXPERIMENTAL-80 Kansas City, MO ...............913 676-3613
ONLINE Kansas City, MO...ON-LINE Comp Center ....913 341-7987
ONLINE Mission, KS ...Dickinson's Movie Guide  ......913 432-5544
PMS Kansas City, MO...Apple Bits .................913 341-3502*24
RCP/M RBBS Mission, KS...MUG .................913 362-9583*24
NYBBLES-80 Elmsford, NY  .......................914 592-5385
RCP/M RBBS Brewster, NY ........................914 259-5693
RCP/M SJBBS Bearsville, NY  .....................914 679-6559-rb
ST80-PBB Monroe, NY...Monroe Camera Shop ........914 782-7605
ABBS El Paso, TX ...............................915 533-6255
ABBS El Paso, TX ...............................915 533-7039
FORUM-80 El Paso, TX  ...........................915 755-1000*24
NET-WORKS El Paso, TX  .........................915 593-6655
RCP/M El Paso, TX ..............................915 598-6274
Aviators Bulletin Board Sacramento, CA  ...........916 393-4459
BULLET-80 Tulsa, OK  ............................918 749-0059*24
CONNECTION-80 Tulsa, OK .......................918 747-1310*24
```

INDEX

Fred Stern

Dr. Fred Stern has worked in the areas of computer and video graphics, software and quality assurance, mathematical modeling and real time system design and analysis for over 20 years. He has served as the Assistant Director of the University of Rhode Island Computer Center and as a Faculty member of the University of Maryland and New York University. He is presently the President of Fourth Generation Systems, a consulting and educational organization working on state-of-the-art personal computing applicatons.

Stern has a PhD in Chemical Engineering, and is widely published. He has an international reputation as an educator and consultant, and lectures frequently.

More Useful & Entertaining Books from John Muir Publications

How to Keep Your Honda Car Alive
by Fred Cisin & Jack Parvin (14.00)

How to Keep Your VW Rabbit Alive
by Richard Sealey (15.00)

How to Keep Your Volkswagen Alive
by John Muir (12.50)

Flea Market America: A Bargain Hunter's Guide
by Cree McCree (8.50)

The People's Guide to Mexico
(Revised) by Carl Franz (10.50)

The People's Guide to Camping in Mexico
by Carl Franz (10.00)

The On and Off the Road Cookbook
by Carl Franz and Lorena Havens (8.50)

A Guide to Midwifery: Heart and Hands
by Elizabeth Davis (9.00)

A Guide to Dying at Home
by Deborah Duda (7.50)

The Art of Running
by Michael Schreiber (9.00)

The Food and Heat Producing Solar Greenhouse
(Revised) by Bill Yanda & Rick Fisher (8.00)

The Bountiful Solar Greenhouse
by Shane Smith (8.00)

The Guitar Owner's Manual
by Will Martin (6.95)

Computer-Ease
by Gordon Morrell (6.95)

Postage: Add $1 for postage and handling

Additional copies of *Word Processing & Beyond* may be ordered by filling out the form below and enclosing $9.95 plus $1 postage & handling. Send your order to:

John Muir Publications
P.O. Box 613
Santa Fe, NM 87504